The Uncanny House in Elizabeth Bowen's Fiction

MEDIATED FICTIONS
STUDIES IN VERBAL AND VISUAL NARRATIVES

Series Editors: Artur Blaim and Ludmiła Gruszewska-Blaim

Editorial Board
Antonis Balasopoulos
Joanna Durczak
David Malcolm
Fátima Vieira

VOLUME 11

Olena Lytovka

The Uncanny House in Elizabeth Bowen's Fiction

Bibliographic Information published by the Deutsche Nationalbibliothek
The Deutsche Nationalbibliothek lists this publication in the Deutsche Nationalbibliografie; detailed bibliographic data is available in the internet at http://dnb.d-nb.de.

Library of Congress Cataloging-in-Publication Data
Names: Lytovka, Olena, 1983- author.
Title: The uncanny house in Elizabeth Bowen's fiction / Olena Lytovka.
Description: First edition. | New York : Peter Lang, 2016. | Series: Mediated fictions ; volume II | Includes bibliographical references and index.
Identifiers: LCCN 2015046053| ISBN 9783631670255 | ISBN 9783653061932 (e-book)
Subjects: LCSH: Bowen, Elizabeth, 1899-1973—Criticism and interpretation. | Home in literature. | Uncanny, The (Psychoanalysis), in literature. | Loss (Psychology) in literature. | Psychic trauma in literature. | Perception in literature.
Classification: LCC PR6003.O6757 Z679 2016 | DDC 823/.912—dc23 LC record available at http://lccn.loc.gov/2015046053

This publication was financially supported by the
Marie Sklodowska-Curie University in Lublin.

Cover illustration printed with kind permission of Jerzy Durczak.

Reviewed by Marek Błaszak and Anna Kędra-Kardela.

ISSN 2194-5918
ISBN 978-3-631-67025-5 (Print)
E-ISBN 978-3-653-06193-2 (E-Book)
DOI 10.3726/ 978-3-653-06193-2

© Peter Lang GmbH
Internationaler Verlag der Wissenschaften
Frankfurt am Main 2016
All rights reserved.
Peter Lang Edition is an Imprint of Peter Lang GmbH.

Peter Lang – Frankfurt am Main · Bern · Bruxelles · New York ·
Oxford · Warszawa · Wien

All parts of this publication are protected by copyright. Any utilisation outside the strict limits of the copyright law, without the permission of the publisher, is forbidden and liable to prosecution. This applies in particular to reproductions, translations, microfilming, and storage and processing in electronic retrieval systems.

This publication has been peer reviewed.

www.peterlang.com

Contents

Abbreviations 9

Introduction 11

Chapter 1. The Uncanny in Fiction 15
1. The Concept of the Uncanny 15
   1.1 In the Wake of Jentsch and Freud 15
   1.2 From Gothic Spectre to Modern Anxiety 19
2. The Chronotope of the Uncanny 24
   2.1 The Uncanny in the City Space 26
   2.2 The Uncanny in the Domestic Space 27
   2.3 Uncanny Objects 30
3. The Uncanny and the Self 31
   3.1 Identity Disintegration 31
   3.2 The Place of Memory and Memory of Place 33
   3.3 The Uncanny as a Post-Traumatic Effect 34

Chapter 2. "Homeliness Uprooted": Oppressive
            Abodes in Elizabeth Bowen's Novel
            The House in Paris and Selected Short Stories 39
1. Domestic Space in Bowen 39
   1.1 Semi-Reality of Bowen's Houses 41
   1.2 Time and Narration: The Uncanny Return 46
      1.2.1 The Epiphanic "Now" 48
      1.2.2 In Search of the Lost Time 52

2. Resisting Domesticization:
   The Uncanny House and Marriage 55

Chapter 3. "Suffering from Reminiscences": Memory and Trauma in Elizabeth Bowen's Novel *The Death of the Heart* and Selected Short Stories 63

1. The Uncanny Aftereffect 63
   - 1.1 Silence, Darkness and Solitude 64
   - 1.2 Landscape and Character 67
2. The Burden of Memory 72
   - 2.1 The Uncanny Reentry of the Past 72
   - 2.2 Disintegrating Homelessness 75
3. Reality in a Dream or a Dream-like Reality 79
   - 3.1 The Interpretation of Dreams 79
   - 3.2 Waking from Reality 83
4. The Shadowy Other in Bowen's Short Fiction 86

Chapter 4. The Spectre of the Big House in Elizabeth Bowen's Novel *A World of Love* and Selected Short Stories 93

1. The Big House Tradition 93
   - 1.1 Big House fiction 94
   - 1.2 Big House Short Fiction 97
2. The Big House in *A World of Love* 103
   - 2.1 Uncanniness of the Houses: Insecurity and Troubling uncertainty 104
   - 2.2 The Phantoms of the Big House 109

2.3	Space and Time Relations in the Novel	112
2.4	The Inhabitants and Their Trauma	115

Conclusion 123

Bibliography..127

Index...139

Abbreviations

The following abbreviations are used in this book. Details of publication are to be found in the Bibliography.

Elizabeth Bowen

LS	*The Last September* (1929)
HP	*The House in Paris* (1935)
DH	*The Death of the Heart* (1938)
BC	*Bowen's Court* (1942)
WL	*A World of Love* (1955)
CS	*The Collected Stories of Elizabeth Bowen*
BOS	*The Bazaar and Other Stories*

Introduction

Elizabeth Bowen occupies a special place among twentieth-century writers. A superb novelist and a master of short story, she is known for her exquisite style and unconventional narrative technique. For the deep psychological insight she demonstrates in her works, Bowen has been called the "anatomist of consciousness" (Ellmann 2003, xi), the "historian and custodian of memory" (McCarthy, x). Her fiction has been considered in the light of modernist experimentalism and realist innovation, Gothic tradition and gender studies. Nevertheless, without doubt, her contribution to world literature has been considerably underestimated. In critical accounts, for a long time, Bowen's fiction has been overshadowed by the achievements of James Joyce, Virginia Woolf and other canonical writers of the time.

Born in Dublin in 1899, heiress of a Big House in the south of Ireland, Elizabeth Bowen belonged to Anglo-Irish Protestant Ascendancy but spent a great part of her life in England. Her literary sensibilities were largely influenced by the ambiguities of her cultural identity as well as by her disintegrating childhood, fractured by her father's mental illness and her mother's early death, and by witnessing the two most horrible wars of the previous century. Thus, the world of Bowen's protagonists is never secure, never defined; men and women in her novels and short-stories become hostages of their memories which keep returning and haunting them in most disturbing ways. The uncanny atmosphere becomes one of the elements that distinguishes Bowen's fiction from the work of other great writers and makes her prose magnetic and gripping for readers.

In the last decade, Bowen's fiction has been attracting more and more attention of the scholars, partially due to the reconsideration of the place of women writers in modern literature and the development of Irish studies. Among the bulk of research on Bowen's fiction of the last ten years, there are books and articles written by Maud Ellmann (2003), Neil Corcoran (2004), Anna Kędra-Kardela (2003, 2005, 2010), Eibhear Walshe (2009), Vera Kreilkamp (2009), Bethany Chafin (2011), Luke Thurston (2012, 2013) and others. The theses published on Bowen and her prose include the works by Pauline Morgan (2003), Esther Rey Torrijos (2004), Katy Alexandra Menczer (2006), Jessica Gildersleeve (2009), D. V. Lavlinski (2011), etc. Still, many aspects of Bowen's work have been neglected in these and earlier studies and some of her fiction works, in spite of their high literary value, have received very little or no interest.

The present book is part of the new wave of criticism which seeks to reread Bowen's work in a new light. It takes into consideration previous findings and offers a new look at Bowen's fiction, putting the house into the focus of investigation and revealing its key role in the creation of the atmosphere of uncanniness, which is so characteristic of Bowen's fiction. In her novels and short stories, Bowen conveys an acute sense of "where" and "when". She seems to be very conscious of location and of the power of the house within the landscape but the particularity of her style relies on locating the house simultaneously in the present and the past, blurring the borders between now and then and, most of all, on making the house a reflection of her characters' disintegration of identity.

Like many other modernist novelists, Bowen attempts to reimagine death and to reconsider losses that it inevitably yields. In her fiction, there is a recognition of both the need and impossibility of understanding the past, the longing and the failure to assimilate its painful experiences. The protagonists of Bowen's novels and short stories are distressed and disoriented individuals attacked by their own memory. The traumatic experiences of the past shatter the construction of their identity and plunge them into a state of existential crisis with the sense of uncanniness persisting. Therefore, psychoanalysis seems to be the most appropriate instrument for exploration of trauma and Freud's theories to be crucial to the reconceptualisation of death and loss in Bowen's work.

The object of the present study is the uncanny (Germ.: das Unheimliche) in the domestic space of Elizabeth Bowen's fiction. The purpose of the study is to examine the image of the house in Bowen's prose and to analyse its uncanniness in relation to the characters' identity. Taking Freud's essay "The 'Uncanny'" as a starting point and relying on the works of Gaston Bachelard, Michel Foucault and Nicholas Royle, the study provides a psychoanalytic reading of three of Bowen's novels and a selection of her short fiction in order to rethink the position of her work in relation to literary theory, with particular emphasis on time and space relations and the identity of the characters. As far as I am aware, this has not been previously attempted in any exhaustive way.

Chapter One presents the theoretical framework of the study. It relies on the concept of the uncanny, traced back to the works of Freud, Jentsch, Heidegger, Royle and other scholars of the twentieth century. According to Freud, the uncanny is defined as something familiar, but foreign at the same time, resulting in a feeling of it being uncomfortably strange, a feeling of not-being-at-home or a feeling of danger. At the same time, as Jentsch suggests, it presupposes a cognitive dissonance, an uncertainty about the surrounding world, but mostly about oneself. In addition to that, as Freedman points out, the uncanny turns out to be the double figure of repression and return.

Furthermore, the chapter draws on etymological roots of the term and explores its place and meaning in the Gothic and modernist literary traditions underlining the conceptual change the notion underwent in the twentieth century. It also explores the role of the uncanny in time and space relations of a work of fiction and suggests that uncanny space should be viewed as a heterotopian portal where temporality and spatiality collapse.

Finally, the chapter argues that the uncanny is the product of characters' psychological trauma and the crisis of the self. The traumatic experience of characters' past contributes to their identity disintegration and makes them see the world and themselves differently, feel the danger and unfriendliness of the environment and be haunted by the memories of the past. It is thus concluded that the uncanny must be analysed through the perspective of characters' consciousness.

Chapter Two explores the centrality of home for Bowen's fiction and argues that the house, in Bowen, is a liminal space which is positioned in a liminal time. The chapter dwells on the unhomely nature of the house in Bowen's fiction and emphasizes the connection between the house and the inner world of characters, the former being the representation of the latter.

The second chapter focuses on Bowen's novel *The House in Paris* and the short stories "The Needlecase", "Story Scene", "Making Arrangements" and "The Return". It argues that the houses represented in these works of fiction are positioned in a semi-real world where objects seem to be animated while the inhabitants play the passive role of dolls. This uncanny transformation becomes possible due to the personal crises the characters undergo, the crises which make them feel not at home with themselves. Not only do they appear to be trapped in their oppressive abodes, but also in a certain time of their lives, which appears to be most traumatic for them. Having once faced death, orphanhood or adultery, the characters keep coming back to the painful events in their memories, projecting their fears and dissatisfactions onto the house.

The chapter also demonstrates that, in Bowen, time is represented as duration, a flow with no beginning and no end, and Bowen's fiction is often built according to a circular narrative structure. This fact may well suggest that, as far as female characters are concerned, the uncanniness of the house stands for a repressed desire to break away from everydayness, domesticization and to escape "the doll's house" which often meant a site of oppression for women of the first half of the twentieth century. Thus, the end of Chapter Two is devoted to the discussion of gender issues in relation to the house in Bowen.

Chapter Three considers the relationships between the character and the environment and suggests that, in Bowen, the landscape appears to be a part of the character and not vice versa, as was stated by critics before. It is shown that the representation of the house is the correlative of the inhabitants' psychological condition and constitutes a manifestation of the characters' disturbed mental state caused by their memories of the past.

The chapter looks at Bowen's novel *The Death of the Heart* and her short stories "The Apple Tree", "Home for Christmas", "The Cassowary" and "The Shadowy Third". In these texts, the tragic events of the past, seemingly buried and forgotten, haunt the houses but primarily the people who live there. Bowen's characters are, as Freud says "suffering from reminiscences": they are possessed by the past, and the uncanniness they feel is the result of their painful memories. Through an exploration of the protagonists' dreams and fantasies, the chapter discloses the trauma they experience as a result of homelessness, orphanhood, exile or the death of a dear person.

Chapter Four reads Bowen's novel *A World of Love* and her short stories "Her Table Spread", "Sunday Afternoon", "Christmas Games" and "The Claimant" in terms of their belonging to the Anglo-Irish Big House tradition. The Irish Big House is the major setting and a major symbol in these works of fiction, which means that among the most common motifs there is isolation and decay but at the same time an acute sense of belonging to the place and extreme attachment to property. This chapter considers the ways in which uncertainty and ambiguity in the matter of ownership can disintegrate the characters' self. It also dwells upon the troubled sexuality of the inhabitants of the Big House, their unexpressed or hidden desires and unrealized, "unconsummated" love.

The fourth chapter argues that Bowen's Big House fiction is not necessarily concerned with national historical trauma, as was shown by other scholars. The losses Bowen's characters experience in these texts are not framed within socio-political trauma but within personal psychological injury. The images of death and decay crystallize around the house turning it into a symbol of loss.

The conclusion recapitulates the findings of the study. It states that the uncanniness of Bowen's houses comes from the traumatic experience of the characters, particularly from the experiences of orphanhood, homelessness and the death of a dear person. The traumatic experience of the loss causes uncertainty about the characters' identity, a crisis of their self, which, in its turn, appears to be the reason for space and time fragmentation and the uncanniness of the house in Bowen.

Chapter 1. The Uncanny in Fiction

> *The uncanny as it is depicted in literature, in stories and imaginative productions, merits in truth a separate discussion.*[1]

1. The Concept of the Uncanny

1.1 In the Wake of Jentsch and Freud

The starting point for my investigation is the work of Ernst Jentsch and Sigmund Freud, who significantly contributed to the development of the concept of the uncanny not only in the field of psychology but very largely in philosophy, literary studies, cultural studies and other fields.

Jentsch was one of the first scholars who began to investigate the concept of the uncanny (Germ. unheimlich – "un-home-like"). He concerned himself with describing from the psychological point of view the mechanism and the causes of the emergence of the uncanny feeling. Jentsch claimed that the impression of uncanniness is in the first place caused by the lack of orientation. In his opinion, "unheimlich" presupposes cognitive dissonance, intellectual uncertainty about the surrounding world, but mostly about oneself; the merging of sensations such as "old/known/familiar" and "new/foreign/hostile" results in the sensation of uncertainty and disorientation.

According to Jentsch, the uncanny effect can be produced by an obscure doubt whether something inanimate is alive or vice versa. The sight of moving automata or motionless wax figures can fill one with a feeling of terror. Especially in the dark, people can reinterpret harmless things as terrifying. Manifestations of mental and nervous illnesses can also cause the uncanny feeling. For instance, a fit of epilepsy may produce a demonic effect on those who are not used to see it. A dead body may inflict horror on people as well.

Jentsch claims that these manifestations can give the impression of a mechanism artwork, thus confusing the spectator. The uncanny effect is produced because this confusion is not conscious and the disorientation is concealed. One

---

[1] Sigmund Freud, "The 'Uncanny'". *The Standard Edition of the Complete Psychological Works of Sigmund Freud.* Trans. James Strachey, with Anna Freud, Alix Strachey and Alan Tyson. *Volume XVII (1917–1919): An Infantile Neurosis and Other Works* (London: Hogarth Press and the Institute of Psycho-Analysis, 1986), p. 218.

of the reasons – ignorance – is more characteristic of children. Another reason is the subjective perception of vacillation: "But one's insight can be especially reduced because of a rampantly proliferating fantasy, as a consequence of which reality becomes mixed up in a more or less conscious way with the additions of the apperceiving brain itself. In the latter case, confusion must of course be the result in how one regards things and, equally, in how one intervenes appropriately in one's environment" (Jentsch, 10).

The feeling of being threatened by something unknown and incomprehensible arises because of the lack of orientation with respect to one's psychical processes. According to Jentsch, women and children are particularly subject to the uncanny feeling because of the more developed fantasy and affectively prevailed psychical background, although, in general man has a tendency to consider things in the external world to be animate in the same way as he is.

Jentsch considers "foreign" to be the key notion as far as the uncanny is concerned. It means that something that is uncanny is or seems to be foreign. However, this impression is subjective; moreover, it does not necessarily invoke an uncanny effect in everybody and every time: "In any case, a stronger tendency to bring about such sensations of uncertainty under certain external circumstances is created in the case of an abnormal disposition or merely a psychical background deriving from an abnormal base, as for example in light sleep, states of deadening of all kinds, various forms of depression and after-effects of diverse terrible experiences, fears, and severe cases of exhaustion or general illness" (Jentsch, 11).

Freud disagrees with Jentsch's point of view and denies the key role of intellectual uncertainty as far as the uncanny is concerned: "Jentsch's point of an intellectual uncertainty has nothing to do with the effect" (Freud 1986, 230). Like Jentsch, Freud analyses E. T. A. Hoffmann's story *The Sand Man* and also other works of fiction but concludes that Jentsch's theory is incapable of explaining the nature of the uncanny. Freud applies the psychoanalytical method and he sees the effect in the anxiety caused by infantile complexes or prehistoric beliefs. Or, as Ellen Peel summarizes it, the uncanny feeling – in literature or life – results from a psychological disorder in the perceiver (410).

In his attempts to define the uncanny Freud asserts that it is "undoubtedly related to what is frightening – to what arouses dread and horror" (1986, 219). He looks into the etymology of the word "unheimlich" inferring that its meaning may be the opposite of "Heimlich" ("homely", "familiar", "intimate", "friendly"). Comparing the meaning of "umheimlich" in different languages Freud obtains the synonymic row: suspicious-strange-foreign-uncomfortable-uneasy-gloomy-dismal-ghastly-haunted-sinister-demonic-gruesome.

However, the meaning of "Heimlich" as "belonging to a house" and "homely" is only its first meaning. As Freud discovers, in its second meaning "Heimlich" means "concealed", "secret", "magic", "mystic", "unconscious". Freud reveals that "unheimlich" is not actually the opposite of it. The meanings of the two words overlap: "Thus *heimlich* is a word the meaning of which develops in the direction of ambivalence, until it finally coincides with its opposite, *unheimlich*. *Unheimlich* is in some way or other a sub-species of *Heimlich*" (Freud 1986, 226). Thus "unheimlich" is at the same time related to a house and to something concealed.

According to Freud, the uncanny must have an element of danger in it. It may be something domestic but at the same time unfriendly, dangerous, something that sets the sense of insecurity within the four walls of one's house. Persons, things, sense-impressions, experiences and situations which are known and long familiar arouse in us the feeling of danger, fear and even horror. Everyday objects may suddenly lose their familiar side, and become messengers. On the whole, the uncanny is something that can be familiar, yet foreign at the same time, resulting in a feeling of it being uncomfortably strange or uncomfortably familiar, a feeling of not-being-at-home.

Among the themes of uncanniness Freud brings forward the idea of "the double", which includes identical looking characters, telepathy, double identity and involuntary repetition or recurrence of the same situation. In early times, the "double" had a positive meaning of multiplication, preservation against destruction or death. Freud suggests that the uncanny feeling is related to the figure of a "double" and people's unconscious "compulsion to repeat" (1986, 236).

Another situation that can arouse in us the feeling of uncanniness is a coincidence and, finally, the so-called "omnipotence of thoughts". The latter convinces Freud that everything perceived as uncanny finds its expression because of residues of animistic mental activity within us. Thus, the scholar comes to the conclusion that the uncanny is constituted by something repressed which recurs, no matter if it is something causing fear or a different emotion. The uncanny is not something new, but something old and familiar repressed and so alienated. It is secretly familiar.

Besides involuntary repetitions, the omnipotence of thoughts and animism – the main factors which can render something uncanny – Freud also mentions magic and sorcery, man's attitude to death and the idea of being buried alive by mistake.

Darkness, silence and solitude are also closely connected with the uncanny and are factors producing the uncanny effect. Silence and darkness stand for a secret. Silence may be interpreted as an unspoken element, something withheld or omitted (consciously or unconsciously). Darkness anticipates disclosure: "it is not so much darkness itself (whatever that might be), but the process of ceasing to be dark, the process of revelation or bringing to light, that is uncanny" (Royle 2003b, 108). It is what comes out of the darkness.

There are other elements determining the production of the feeling of uncanniness but, according to Freud, they all originate in not fully surmounted beliefs of prehistoric people or in repressed infantile complexes revived by some impression.

Laurie Ruth Johnson combines Jentsch's and Freud's approaches and defines the uncanny as "an experience of frightening disorientation that is repetitive and reminds us of repetition itself" (9). On the one hand, Johnson agrees with Jentsch's point of view that the uncanny has to do with the lack of orientation, but on the other hand, like Freud, she admits its repetitive character.

Johnson claims that the uncanny effect is produced as a result of an encounter with something strangely familiar. It can function as a kind of liberation, an intersection of pain and pleasure. The anxiety, fear, disorientation can be painful and destructive on a personal level, although the pleasure may consist in revealing, bringing to consciousness the unconscious ideas. "Uncanny encounters, which occur when something strangely familiar evokes a repressed affect and provokes anxiety, remind us of something lost; we thus re-experience the loss" (Johnson 2010, 29). The repetition here means re-experiencing.

Martin Heidegger explores the concept of the uncanny in terms of existentialism. According to him, uncanniness means not-being-at-home, which must be considered as a primordial phenomenon: "uncanniness is the fundamental kind of being-in-the-world" (Heidegger, 256). The uncanny is feared, thus it must be threatening and potentially harmful. The uncanny is related to the feeling of anxiety and is connected with death (a flight from the uncanniness is a flight from being-toward-death). Like Freud, Heidegger admits the uncanny character of silence. He connects the uncanny with home, familiarity, concealment and unconcealment, truth uncovering.

Heidegger discusses the uncanniness in terms of everyday, familiar being-in-the-world and everyday familiarity collapse. He claims that the threat of uncanniness goes along with complete security and self-sufficiency of the everyday way of taking care of things. There is no need of darkness, the uncanny can arise in the most harmless situations. In addition, the uncanny is often psychologically conditioned. The threat concerns Da-sein but it comes from Da-sein itself. Therefore the subject can feel the uncanny only when the uncanny is triggered by himself/herself. In order to interpret uncanniness, thus, it is necessary to turn to the individual consciousness.

Jo Collins and John Jervis also point out that it is characteristic of the uncanny to play across the boundaries (internal/external, self/other) (Collins, Jervis, 4). The uncanny belongs to the borderline, an uneasy zone between two states. Tzvetan Todorov presents the uncanny as the experience of limits (46). It is linked with the collapse of the limit between the self and the other, life and death, real and fantastic.

Summing it up, the concept of the uncanny includes the key notions of home, foreignness, everydayness, revelation and encounter with the otherness, boundary and liminality. The uncanny is the experience of alienation through suppression. It must be analysed through the perspective of individual consciousness.

1.2 From Gothic Spectre to Modern Anxiety

Manifestations of the uncanny par excellence are well known to researchers of the Gothic. Gothic fiction or supernatural fiction, weird fiction, horror fiction, fantasy fiction, vampire literature, ghost stories and other genres and sub-genres may claim their rights to the invention of the uncanny.

Houses haunted by ghosts, curses, madness, vampires, monsters, detached body parts, being buried alive and other themes have appeared in literature for centuries. The Gothic novel usually deals with the dark themes in human nature against medieval background and with elements of the supernatural. Magic, hallucinations, corpses, tombs, demons are often present in Gothic fiction. Its prominent features include mystery, secrets, darkness, the supernatural, and its effect feeds on a pleasing sort of terror.

One of the most frequent motifs relying on the supernatural is the apparition of a ghost or a spectre. The spectre, as Jacques Derrida points out, is "the visibility of the invisible" (125). It is "what one imagines, what one thinks one sees and which one projects – on an imaginary screen where there is nothing to see" (Derrida, 125). It is the vision that returns, becomes frequent. What is more, Derrida claims that the ghost or the spectre first sees us, before we can see it. It engenders the feeling of being observed, under surveillance. The spectre appears at the intersection and that makes it uncanny.

Motifs with uncanny connotations including the spectre are automatically included into the Gothic. But is the Gothic uncanny identical to that in modernist fiction?

Terry Castle claims that the eighteenth century "invented the uncanny" following the invention of automata (8). It is undeniable that some modernist writers exhibit Gothic tendencies. Gothic literature has influenced and inspired modernists and it seems likely that the origins of the modernist uncanny are in the Gothic. But although themes of the Gothic novel and the modernist novel may in many cases overlap, the devices they employ and the effect they produce differ considerably.

The master category of the Gothic is the sublime (Bomarito, 1–2), which differs considerably from the uncanny. The sublime is an aesthetic quality in opposition to beauty referring to the experience of pleasure mingled with repulsion or the experience of an agreeable kind of horror. It also has to do with crossing boundaries and going beyond the limits (Ellison, 53, 133, 173). The sublime may inspire horror, but one receives pleasure in knowing that it is a fiction.

As for the uncanny, it is not about the pleasure of being frightened but the disintegration of the certainty about the world. The uncanny "would be characterized better as "dread" than terror, deriving its force from its very inexplicability, its sense of lurking unease, rather than from any clearly defined source of fear – an uncomfortable sense of haunting rather than a present apparition" (Vidler, 23). The uncanny in modernism is the negation of the boundaries of reality, questioning of what is aesthetic, provoking the reflection if and in what way one can distinguish between fiction and reality in the modern world.

The Gothic novel is characterized by intricate but often loosely constructed plots, stock characters such as a young woman and a lascivious male villain, and a medieval setting, such as a haunted, ruined castle (Bomarito, 231). A ghost in a Gothic novel would most likely be an apparition of a person who died a violent death or committed suicide and would haunt the offender or the place of grief. In a modernist novel, ghostliness does not necessarily apply to human beings but very often to places, events, impressions, attitudes revived again and again by the memory. The representation of the uncanny has undergone an apparent evolution since the rise of the Gothic. The eighteenth-century Gothic shifted from plainly depicting ghostly phenomena toward character psychology in the nineteenth century and was crowned with psychoanalysis in the twentieth century.

According to David Ellison, modernism cannot be studied independently of its figuration in the uncanny (53). Uncanniness inhabits the works of many modernist writers, and its reverberations are present in the fiction of Marcel Proust, Franz Kafka, Joseph Conrad, André Gide, Virginia Woolf and many others. Modernity is "traumatized by conflict and wracked by doubt" (Matz, 7). And as Nicholas Royle claims, the uncanny is a key to understanding modernity and psychoanalysis is crucial to such understanding.

Modernism is centered on the inner life of the character. As Marlowe Miller puts it, "[m]odernists turned to interiority and a world of private symbolization as the focus of art" (2006, 3). For modernists the world lost stability, and at the same time there was "a loss of confidence in the stability of identity" (Miller 2006, 4). Moreover, the beginning of the 20th century brought about the challenge to gender roles and the bounds of sexuality. In their writings, modernists sought to reflect the instability of modern existence and the elusive human nature.

The new style relied on fragments, breaks, ellipses and disrupted linearity of the narration. It served to convey the idea of the fractured character of modern time and fragmentariness and allusiveness of subconscious thought. Freud's critique of the classical concept of the self was very popular at the time and many writers demonstrated their awareness and admiration of psychoanalysis.

The new age proclaimed a new manner of being, bringing the individual into a state of deep inner fragmentation. In the new fictional discourse writers tended to depict the new character, "psychologically deep and multi-layered, fragmentary, floating on sensation and consciousness, fed by their random thoughts and their halfconscious dream worlds" (Bradbury, 153). Thus, the uncanny appeared to be what Maria M. Tatar calls "an externalization of consciousness" (167).

At the beginning of the 20th century the concepts of space and time became "subjectivized" (Kershner, 57). Einstein's theory of relativity and Bergson's concept of duration which conveyed the meaning of experienced time were vividly exemplified in the works of modernist writers such as Marcel Proust, James Joyce, Virginia Woolf and others. In the modernists, there was a tendency towards "time consciousness" which was the longing "to collapse meaning into an instance of time" (Kershner, 58).

Modernist fiction tended to represent a meta-world which was not characterized by linearity and continuity, with its leaps in time, gaps or temporal irregularity. The classical categories of time and space had been changed. Time became more elastic and the moment in the present could expand and contract depending on the situation, it became a kind of simultaneity containing the past, the present and the future at the same time.

The modernist aesthetics of simultaneity is an attempt to retrieve the lost identity through the work of memory. The epiphanic structure of the narration allows expressing the characters' search for identity through the revelational moments of insight. The central problem of consciousness in modernist literature manifests itself as an attempt at an insight into the self or/and the other. In addition to its epiphanic structure, there are other experimental uses of narration such as the projection of narrators or multiple perspectives which lay the emphasis on the subjectivity on the one hand, but at the same time contribute to the decentralization of the subject in the work of fiction.

The disrupted temporality, the centrality of memory and consciousness issues in modernist fiction make it inseparable with the concept of the uncanny. But what makes the uncanny a master category of modernism is the representation of isolation and alienation of the subject in the modern world which becomes "defamiliarised", foreign to man.

Modernist writers attempt to shatter the world which seems to be safe and full of sense. Their protagonists suddenly discover that the conventional world of objects and relations where they felt themselves at home is eventually not so safe. Modernism as a product of experience of the big city with its cult of technical innovation and experience of the war tries to grasp and show the reader the fundamentally "unhomely" modern condition.

The category of "alienation" is considered to be central to understanding of existence in modernity (Edgar, 314). The uncanny, in its turn, plays a central part in the modernist self-understanding of the contemporary human condition as one of alienation. In modernist fiction, society is depicted as "a paradoxical and tragic community of strangers" (Edgar, 315). The uncanny in modernism is thus largely expressed by means of the artistic device of "defamiliarisation", making the world strange and unfamiliar.

Andrew Edgar emphasizes the etymological link between the concept of "unheimlich" and the notion of homelessness. He concludes that the adult is never fully at home. This unhomelessness is present in the unconscious, and the life and behaviour of man are compromised by repressed anxieties and traumas of separation. "This etymology allows the uncanny to be understood as one of a cluster of categories through which modernity articulated itself, in philosophy and social theory, and in art and literature", points out Edgar (314). He sees the metaphor of homelessness as a key to understanding the uncanny as a manifestation of alienation.

Following Jentsch's idea, Collins and Jervis define the uncanny as an experience of disorientation where the world in which we live suddenly seems strange, alienating or threatening. The uncanny is associated with modernity, moreover, the scholars consider it to be its fundamental, constitutive aspect: "the uncanny has become a key term for figuring the uncertainties, tensions and obscurities of modernity itself" (Collins, Jervis, 5).

Ellison claims that the feeling of uncanniness, of not-being-at-home is the feeling of alienation *per se*. The uncanny is "the domain of death-in-life, a ghostly place or non-place in which the aesthetic and the ethical cross into each other's territories and disrupt the boundaries separating the one sphere from the other" (Ellison, 133). It can mean "the inhuman", "the impersonal". Uncanny landscapes are deserts, islands, cages, walled expanses, underground passageways. Julian Wolfreys adds the labyrinth to the list. But most uncanny, according to Ellison, are places containing reflections of home (158).

According to Harold Bloom, Freud's uncanny *is* alienation, a modern version of the Sublime (2009, xv). Alienation is experienced as a result of isolation, inner conflict and anxiety, the suppression coming from the society and its values and the emptiness which follows.

The uncanny blurs the boundaries of inside and outside, it disrupts the distinction between self-reflection, exploration of the unconscious mind and the "real" world. It complicates differentiation at the level of the narrative structure, the distinction between the outer frame provided by the exterior narrator and the inner frame by particular characters. It contributes to the disruption of narrative boundaries, has to do with the play with language, peculiar word manipulation and repetitions. Andrew Bennett and Nicholas Royle have carried out a linguistic research similar to that of Freud but focusing on the word "familiar". First of all "familiar" goes back to "family" and so to "home" and to the concealed (e. g. "to keep things in the family"). It has the meaning of something known and intimate, one of its meanings presupposing a relation to what is demonic.

The researchers of modernist literature distinguish between thirteen forms of the uncanny: 1) repetition, 2) odd coincidences, 3) animism, 4) anthropomorphism, 5) automatism, 6) a sense of radical uncertainty about sexual identity, 7) a fear of being buried alive, 8) silence, 9) telepathy, 10) death, 11) the death drive, 12) ghosts, 13) language (Bennett, Royle, 36–40). Eight of these forms (1–3, 5, 7–10) can be traced back to the essays of Jentsch and Freud. Anthropomorphism has been put into a separate category as a specific form of animism. So has been the death drive, the form inspired by Freud's essay "Beyond the Pleasure Principle".

Remarkably, language is also considered to be a form of the uncanny. It is bound up with an uncanny feeling when something is unnameable, beyond language, when one deals with the crisis of language. Bennet and Royle suggest that language is foreign by its nature as it is often subject to distortion, censorship, slippage, translation, wordplay, of which we are unaware. But there are also literary devices, tropes applied intentionally by the author to create an uncanny feeling. Very often the text of the modernist novel is haunted by other texts. The ghosts appear in the form of allusions, symbols, recurrent motifs or repeated metaphors. These are also manifestations of the uncanny in modernist literature.

In conclusion, it is clear that the uncanny in modernist literature, although it may own its origin to the Gothic, considerably differs from it. The modernist uncanny is interrelated with the disrupted linearity and aesthetics of simultaneity characteristic of modernist fiction. It relies on the centrality of consciousness, memory and identity search topics and is determined by the alienation as a human condition of the world. The new style and experiments with narration and language in general contributed to producing more of the uncanny effect in modernist fiction than in any earlier epoch.

2. The Chronotope of the Uncanny

Temporal and spatial relationships are interrelated and interdependent, and it would certainly be wrong to consider one without the other. The interconnection of time and space in literature is the subject that has enjoyed much interest among scholars. One of them, Mikhail Bakhtin, introduces the concept of "chronotope". He defines it as "the intrinsic connectedness of temporal and spatial relationships that are artistically expressed in literature" (Bakhtin, 84). Bakhtin insists on their inseparability and views time as the fourth dimension of space. He claims that the artistic chronotope is characterized by the intersection of time and space axes and fusion of their indicators, with time being the dominant category in the chronotope.

On the other hand, Michel Foucault regards space as dominant in the fusion: "In any case I believe that the anxiety of our era has to do fundamentally with space, no doubt a great deal more than with time. Time probably appears to us only as one of the various distributive operations that are possible for the elements that are spread out in space" (Foucault). No matter which point of view may be adopted, there is no doubt that the uncanny must be studied in both its temporal and spatial aspects.

The temporal side of the uncanny is disclosed as a disquieting return of the past or revisited past, risen up again when seemingly put to rest. Therefore, Jervis dwells upon the category of "presence". The experience of an obscure feeling of the presence of something or somebody can be uncanny. This presence is inevitably linked with the past and involves remembering the images of the past. The images disturb us, make us fear the present because of the presence of the past in it. "It disturbs deeply held, taken-for-granted assumptions about what is real and unreal, or imaginary, about the world, and the entities within it; whether these entities are dead or alive, animate or inanimate, natural or artificial, self or other. And hence one can be disturbed by something, even when one is not necessarily sure that there is a 'something' there to be disturbed by" (Jervis, 11). The boundaries become blurred and the experience is perceived as neither inside nor outside, caught between past and present, material and immaterial, real and unreal.

Time in modernist fiction is often represented as the emergence of the past in the present with its sudden revelations, epiphanies uncovering the concealed truth and bringing it to light. Epiphany is "the description of the sudden flare into revelation of an ordinary object or scene" (Abrams, 81). Robert Langbaum characterizes it by psychological association, momentousness, suddenness and fragmentation (44). Epiphanies have become a constructive principle of modern fiction. The moments "taken out of the ordinary time flow", "flashes", "suddenly appearing images" are characteristic of the modernist narrative pattern (Nycz, 43). They are grounded in the ordinary, domestic, trivial but possess considerable performative power.

The uncanny effect is often achieved at these moments when time is suspended, frozen. These sudden manifestations of secretly familiar or unconsciously forgotten truths are inherent in the uncanny, which is also confirmed in the quotation from Schelling: "Unheimlich is the name for everything that ought to have remained ... secret and hidden but has come to light" (Freud 1986 after Schelling, 225). Like epiphany, the uncanny is always experiential.

In terms of the uncanny there is always an encounter as a reminder, a memory coming from the other, the unconscious, revealing strange otherness. The encounter with alterity is epiphanic. This experience takes one out of the everyday. Something happens between the place and the experience of place. The uncanny always takes "place". A striving to relive the past not only causes a temporal dislocation, but a recurrence from the past disrupts the space.

The fragmentation of time contributes to the fragmentation of space as well. The uncanny space appears to be very "heterotopian" – containing in itself the multiplicity of spaces. According to Foucault, the space people live in is not homogeneous or empty, it is heterogeneous. Foucault introduces the term "heterotopias", equivalent to "real places [...] which are something like counter-sites", "[p]laces of this kind are outside of all places, even though it may be possible to indicate their location in reality" (Foucault). Heterotopias are places containing many other places within themselves. An example of heterotopia may be the ancient garden. Gardens which could boast plants brought from overseas countries, statues made by ancient sculptors and recreating the atmosphere of bygone epochs represent multiple worlds in one world. Similarly, one may regard the modern city as a heterotopia, with its multiethnic quarters, older and newer parts, monuments and street names commemorating various past events. Home may be heterotopian too.

Heterotopias are most often linked to slices in time – heterochronies. Foucault thinks that the heterotopia starts fully functioning when one arrives at an absolute break with traditional time. Being linked to the accumulation of time, heterotopias are also bound to time in its flowing, transitory aspect.

Furthermore, Foucault singles out crisis heterotopias, which are "privileged or sacred or forbidden places, reserved for individuals who are, in relation to society and to the human environment in which they live, in a state of crisis: adolescents, menstruating women, pregnant women, the elderly, etc" (Foucault). Thus, heterotopias have to do with boundaries and their crossing. They are a kind of portals into other spaces and times, as they always presuppose a system of opening and closing that isolates them and makes them penetrable at the same time.

Therefore, there is a close relation of the uncanny to the spatial and environmental and its interconnection with that of the temporal. The uncanny suggests an indecision, an obscurity in the sense of time and place. This indecision is unsettling, troubling. The uncanny rises in "that mental space where temporality and spatiality collapse" (Vidler, 39).

2.1 The Uncanny in the City Space

The end of the 19th century brought new experiences of urban modernity. The urban world partially changes the gothic uncanny into the "technological uncanny". The invention of photo, film and phone (with their "disembodied voices" and "disembodied images") and their introduction into use have become resources through which the uncanny presence of a disturbing otherness is revealed. The sense of unease has been associated with modern anxieties, neuroses, especially disturbances of the spatial kind like claustrophobia or agoraphobia.

Among the researchers who study the "urban uncanny" there is Walter Benjamin. He attributes the ghostliness of the city to the multiplicity and juxtaposition of spatial and temporal markers (Benjamin, 516–26). Julian Wolfreys, in the chapter "Citephobia", also treats architectural and topographic spaces as the manifestation of the uncanny producing the feeling of anxiety, not being at home in the city (1998, 95–102). Petra Eckhard, who investigates the uncanny in spatio-temporal relations emphasizes the dark and nightmarish character of modern cities and presents the uncanny as a specifically urban phenomenon (Eckhard, 10).

The uncanniness of the city may reside in its being presented as a zone of liminality: relating to a transitional or initial stage of a process or occupying a position at, or on both sides of, a boundary. The uncanny erases border or limit between the familiar and the unfamiliar, and the city becomes a locus of the isolated subject. In his article "The Urban Uncanny", Wolfreys notes: "The very condition of the uncanny experience, then, is that there is always the inexorable slide, inescapable as well as ineluctable, from the familiar to the unfamiliar, the homely to the unhomely, the 'canny' or 'known' to the 'uncanny'. And this equally has to do with one's 'self', one's identity or being and one's location, where location or context determines who one thinks one is, and how the subject is orientated or disorientated not only in the present but in relation to the past, to personal, and to cultural memory" (2008, 170).

Wolfreys sees the relation between the urban and the uncanny through the idea of home – "dwelling", "building", "house". This part of the urban space is worth most thorough consideration.

2.2 The Uncanny in the Domestic Space

The haunted house, a pervasive leitmotiv of Gothic novels, as Anthony Vidler puts it, is a popular topos of the twentieth-century uncanny: "The house provided an especially favored site for uncanny disturbances: its apparent domesticity, its residue of family history and nostalgia, its role as the last and most intimate shelter of private comfort sharpened by contrast the terror of invasion by alien spirits" (Vidler, 17).

The saying "An Englishman's home is his castle" suggests that domestic space is usually associated with safety, reliability and stability. Nevertheless, very often it is the home that evokes in its inhabitants the feeling of being under threat. Alanna Lawley introduces the idea of home as a balance between the stable and unstable. Stability is attributed to the home and instability – to the house (Lawley). Lawley notes that continual relocation, moves from house to house, especially in childhood, may influence individual perception of the domestic environment.

But even if the person is settled and seldom moves to other places, the warmth and safety of the domestic space may be ostensible, as the house itself is disturbed by secrets and fears and destabilized by their disclosure. "A home is a place of familiarity where the secrets invariably raise the spectre of taboo and transgression, with their profound consequences for identity" (Jervis, 20). The domestic space can enforce physical and psychological repression on the individual, producing the feeling of being imprisoned.

The analysis of theoretical works on the subject shows that the localization of the uncanny within the domestic permits its decipherment in individual experience. According to Gaston Bachelard, the domestic space represents an inner space, since it embodies the inner world of the subject (6–8). It stands for what is personal, intimate, sometimes hidden from the others. Our domestic space can tell much about us. From the size, location, the way we furnish, decorate and look after the place we live in, one can judge not only about our social status and fortune, but also about our character, taste, hobbies, inclinations, not only about the present, but also about the past. The house is full of marks of our past life, as "to dwell means to leave traces" (Benjamin, 9).

Bachelard combines phenomenology and psychoanalysis in his approach to the house. In his book *The Poetics of Space* he writes: "The house is not experienced from day to day only, on the thread of a narrative, or in the telling of our own story. Through dreams, the various dwelling places in our lives co-penetrate and retain the treasures of former days. And after we are in the new house, when memories of other places we have lived in come back to us, we travel to the land of Motionless Childhood, motionless the way all Immemorial things are" (5–6).

Memories of home differ from memories of the outside world. The former are much more vivid and deeply embedded: "Our memories of former dwelling-places are relived as daydreams that these dwelling-places of the past remain in us for all time" (6). To examine the concept of the domestic space Bachelard applies topoanalysis – psychoanalysis of localization of memories, "the sights of our intimate lives" (8). He claims that memories are fixed in space, they do not record duration. The past is actually fixations in the spaces, and most firmly our memory is fixed on the childhood home. This brings us to Freud and his idea of infantile complexes and fears engendered in early childhood. A shock or an upset the person experiences at home in childhood may lead to his fears as a grown-up.

But Freud goes further in his investigation and seeks for the source of infantile fears. He claims that the fear is in fact a heritage: "Herein the child would only repeat the behavior of prehistoric man and of the primitive man of today who, on account of his ignorance and helplessness, fears everything that is new, and much that is familiar, all of which can no longer inspire us with fear" (Freud 2010, 27). Finally, Freud comes to the conclusion that the child (and later the adult) fears the power of his libido (2010, 28).

The house is a symbol of the human body. All enclosed space, according to Freud, symbolically represents the female genitals, while the room is a representation of the womb of the mother. The flame stands for the male genitals, the fireplace or the hearth for the womb of the woman. The clock, the door, the window also represent the female genitals. Therefore, the fear related to the domestic space appears to be a transformation of unsatisfied libido.

Bachelard's theory partially shares with Freud the idea of the house as a representation of human body. A house is built by and for the body, taking the form of a shell; the house we were born in is "physically inscribed in us" (Bachelard, 14). It is a large cradle, the original warmth, the human being's first world. But, in Bachelard, the house represents the man's body *and* soul (italics mine – O. L.).

Within the primitive imaginary the family house is a shelter, a refuge, a corner where one can hide away. It gives one physical pleasure to withdraw to this corner. The corner is a symbol of solitude, silence and immobility (Bachelard, 137). The house can be imagined as a nest, a chrysalis, concentrated and hermetic. From a casket to a wardrobe, the enclosed space suggests intimacy, a hiding place for people and their secrets. "The hidden in men and the hidden in things belong in the same topoanalysis" (Bachelard, 89).

The form of the house from the inside repeats the form of the body (like a nest or a prehistoric man's house). A nest or a shell can be built only from the inside. "The body, indeed, has become its own exterior, as its cell structure has become the object of spatial modeling" (Vidler, 167). Similarly, the mental image of the house repeats or echoes the inside world of the subject. The image of the house is the imprint of man's mental state.

The house of prehistoric man was round with the fire in the centre. It was the light spot in the darkness of the place. The archetypal image of the light surrounded by the space of the house stresses the concentration of intimacy within it. The light inside of the house is compared to the eye of a creature. And following Freud's dream symbolism, the fear of the darkness or losing the source of light can be related to the castration complex.

The fireplace still functions as a central image of the house. On the other hand, the house is a centre itself, surrounded by the hostility of the world. Therefore, the house must be conceived as an opposition of centre and periphery, interior and exterior.

In Bachelard's *The Poetics of Space* the house is imagined as a concentrated being and as a vertical being. In its dual vertical polarity the roof stands for rationality, the cellar – for irrationality. The cellar represents darkness and depth. It is the unconscious, according to Jung. The fears of the cellar with its buried walls are deeper than the fears of the attic, as the latter can be more easily rationalized. The cellar and the attic acquire the form of double architecture with the space above the ground and a subterranean labyrinth underneath (Vidler, 131).

Jurij Lotman has proposed the spatial category of boundary which can be used in the analysis of the space of the house. In *The Structure of the Artistic Text,* Lotman speaks about the opposition "high-low" along the vertical axis (218–222). In this opposition, "top" stands for "good", "spaciousness", "spirituality", "sky", "life", whereas "bottom" means "evil", "crowding", "materiality", "earth", "death". The downward movement is interpreted as longing for immobility or as predetermined movement; the upward movement is interpreted as free movement, a movement for transformation. What is "near" is identified with what is understandable, familiar, and "distant" is associated with what is alien. "Height" is associated with "distance" and "bottom" is identified with "nearness".

To sum up, the representations of the house and the fears related to its space go back to the fears of childhood and beliefs of prehistoric times. The interpretation of the domestic space relies on the idea of the house as body and soul, reflecting the physical and mental state of the person. The spatial oppositions "high-low", "interior-exterior", "central-peripheral", etc. also play an important role in the analysis.

2.3 Uncanny Objects

Henri Poincaré remarks that space cannot be imagined as empty; in fact, space is objects in space (Poincaré, 51). Therefore, the perception of space is in its essence the perception of objects in it. Quite a few modernist writers exhibit animistic sensibilities and often present inanimate objects as those possessing sentience. They offer the possibility that furniture or other items of domestic interior can register opinions and have relationships with one another, regardless if the human mediator is present or not (Inglesby, 307). Sometimes familiar objects can become alien, hostile and even acquire features of monstrosity.

The connection between the animation of objects and human psyche in literature can hardly be contested. Things are representations of the protagonists' personal life, and houses and their furnishings are human projections onto them. The role things play in the novel is that of mirrors of the protagonists' character or, in a broader view, of their consciousness.

Things are rememberers of the past. They conjure up memories: "their vestments, always slightly faded, and dated, remind us of those who came before; they embody dreams, delusions of presence now past" (Jervis, 18). Furniture and household objects that fill the house are vessels for holding histories that coincide with those maintained by their owners (Inglesby, 314). They are "cherished repositories of memory which embody human emotions and intentions" (Wasson, 113). Moreover, household objects are also repositories of generational continuity and with their damage and destruction, for example during the war, people's selves are damaged.

One of the most powerful objects in the modernist novel is the clock. It is used to stop time, slow it down or speed it up, and very often it is a reminder of the past which cannot be let go. Other important objects connected with the protagonists' personalities and embodying the idea of the double are mirrors, photos, diaries and others.

3. The Uncanny and the Self

3.1 Identity Disintegration

Charles Taylor stresses that twentieth-century art has gone more inward, has tended to explore and to celebrate subjectivity. Moreover, it has explored new recesses of feeling, "entered the stream of consciousness" (Taylor, 456). But this tendency does not mean a turn to the self, but beyond the self, "to a fragmentation of experience which calls our ordinary notions of identity into question" (Taylor, 462). The traditional idea of the unitary self collapses in order to give way to "the flux which moves beyond the scope of control or integration" (Taylor, 462).

The uncanny becomes a meta-concept for modernity. The modern self, the carrier of civilization, is at the same time somehow shadowy and spectral. The self and the mind, which seems to be its governing principle, emerge as "uncanny spaces of doubling and fracture" (Collins, Jervis, 4). Modern selves are haunted. According to Michael Saler, the "unheimlich" nature of modernity is reflected in the sense that the self is not rooted or at home with itself but contains, as Walt Whitman claimed, "multitudes" (Saler, 194). One longs for the quest for oneself and one's world and engages in the uncanny in an attempt at capturing the experience of selfhood.

There may be different cases of identity disintegration evoking the feeling of insecurity within oneself. One of the cases is the uncertainty about sexual identity. In the case of homosexuality the ambivalence and uncertainty are prominent. The writers of queer fiction treat the uncanny as a vehicle for queer representation. Queer theory challenges the concept of a stable sexual identity, encompassing the categories of lesbian, gay and/or transgender (Palmer, 6–7). This ambiguity has uncanny implications.

First of all, queer sexuality implies duplicity. The transsexual or transgender subject can experience the sensation of self-division. On the other hand, the fading of boundaries is visible in terms of overlapping roles. Secondly, for the transsexual the category of foreignness is topical. The body is viewed as alien, conflicting the real self. Thirdly, the unease connected with breaking conventions remains pervasive: homosexual drives which have been repressed insist on returning.

Paulina Palmer argues that the haunted house narrative is used "to explore the disturbing effect that same-sex desire can have on the hetero-patriarchal household" (108). Although public imagination excludes the homosexual from the concept of home, his ghost is present in a latent state in popular imagination.

On the whole, the uncanny has the role of a signifier of excess by challenging the conventional view of reality as unitary, questioning mainstream, "common-sense" versions of it. The self-definition beyond the normative model may become a reason of a conflict with the society and oneself. But besides sexual and gender ambiguity, racial or ethnic border-crossing can also result in disorienting uncertainty about one's identity. Questioning ethnic/national identity is very much characteristic of postcolonial literature but is not limited to it.

Despite its collective character, national identity fulfils an internal function for individuals. A sense of national identity provides a powerful means of defining and locating individual selves in the world. Anthony Smith believes that "[i]t is through a shared, unique culture that we are enabled to know 'who we are' in the contemporary world. By rediscovering that culture we 'rediscover' ourselves, the 'authentic self', or so it has appeared to many divided and disoriented individuals who have had to contend with the vast changes and uncertainties of the modern world" (Smith, 17).

A sudden discovery of one's real ethnic origin which is different from what one was brought up in may have a disintegrating effect on one's identity. Being aware of the nationality one belongs to but having spent one's childhood abroad in a completely different environment may engender confusion, and the state of constantly being at the borderland may have a destructive effect on the sense of the self. A feeling of disempowerment, helplessness occurs and the unity of self-identity becomes vulnerable.

The search for identity or a reintegrated subjectivity occupies a significant place in postcolonial writing in particular. It describes the process of "othering" depicting "the unsettling strangeness that colonized peoples represented" (Boehmer, 75). Under colonialism the identity becomes fragmented, displaced, or discredited and the displacement may become a powerful reason for the loss of identity: "Exile, deracination, urban disorientation, the fragmentation of absolutes, alienation in a variety of different forms, all these defined existence for twentieth-century writers throughout the world, both those from the emergent nations and those based in the colonial centre" (Boehmer, 119).

The individual's drive to seek identity is essential for achieving his/her psychological security (Bloom 1993, 23). When the sense of identity appears to be highly insecure, alienation is necessary, so that the subject realizes himself through losing himself, becomes other to become truly himself. One turns toward the past, trying to find definition of himself/herself. Lena Steveker claims that understanding oneself is only possible through memory, through retrospection (77). Remembering the past is indispensible to form the image of oneself and to reach an understanding of oneself.

3.2 The Place of Memory and Memory of Place

Everyone is held captive by memories, which return him/her to a specific place and time. Unconsciously, the places we inhabit or pass through come back to us in the present, sometimes creating a sense of familiarity in the midst of uncertainty. Dylan Trigg believes that every place has a memory. Memories are attributed to the place in our mind. The present can be sensed in the place: sounds, smells contribute to it as well as images. Like Poincaré, Trigg thinks that place is to be understood experientially, as a product of human experience. Places are defined in their relationship with the subject who experiences them, they are situated in between the world and the subject. And things that make up a given place lose their status as "objects" in the world and become an extension of the formal structure of personal identity (Trigg, 9).

The material environment shapes the content of remembering and thus our concept of selfhood. The place of memory is taken as a particular mode of materiality, like monuments and sites of trauma. Memory of the past depends on remembering how things were and reworking that memory in the present. "Just as memory is inherently spatial, so spatiality is inherently temporal, occupying a place in the present but stretching back into the past" (Trigg, xvii).

As we have a body, we necessarily have a relationship with the places that surround us. Those places define and structure our sense of self, so that being displaced can have a dramatic consequence on our experience of who we are, and even leave us with a feeling of being homeless in the world. The materiality of the environment becomes constitutive of who one is. The place is central in our reflective conception of the self. We carry places with us. For instance, to cross the borderline entering a house you have been to before is more than to transgress a spatial border but to enter a different time scale. It means combining traces of familiarity with the presence of unfamiliarity.

An encounter with an unfamiliar place can invoke in us a manifold response, and its origin is not only traceable to the objective features of the place, such as light, heat, and atmosphere. The place invokes an intermingling of different sensations in the body. Unable to define the precise orientation of the body's stirrings, the visitor to the place is left with only a vague sense of uncertainty if not anxiety. As Lawley notes, "[i]t is through the visitors' consciousness of oneself in space and the way in which one perceives reality and its atmosphere that apprehension and the Uncanny arises" (Lawley, 8). In the conjunction of body and place, something of the past is aroused, but it is not clear enough what it is, it must be deciphered by means of psychological analysis.

3.3 The Uncanny as a Post-Traumatic Effect

As Roger Luckhurst assumes, the wound is characteristic for modernity. The contemporary subject is a distressed and disoriented individual attacked by his own memory (128). Remarkably, the human psyche is organized in such a way that, by nature, one tends to forget traumatic or difficult episodes of life. But these episodes do not completely disappear from memory. They blink, provoke the feeling of *déjà vu* or the feeling of being haunted. The uncanny effect appears when something affecting one's senses (something one sees, hears, feels, smells, etc.) forces one to remember what one does not want to remember and to experience the ambivalence by staying in the state of psychological division.

According to Freud, the uncanny is related to knowledge one would rather forget (1986, 241). It has undergone repression and returned in a transformed shape, rendering it strange and terrifying. Consequently, the source of the fear appears to be within the self, not coming from the outer world. In *Beyond the Pleasure Principle,* Freud explains that mental processes are regulated by "the pleasure principle": in their lives, people strive for avoidance of "pain" or production of pleasure (51). That is why the traumatic episodes are forced to be forgotten, ousted from the conscious mind and appear in a disguised form. The original event is distorted to the unconscious mind and is inaccessible to reflection.

Through repression the person experiences difficulty in relinquishing the past and its oppressive history. Nevertheless, the dream life takes one back to the situation of one's disaster. It happens because the person has undergone a psychical fixation on the trauma. Henceforth, one's dreams, fantasies, and one's behaviour is actually remembering the forgotten and the repressed.

According to Freud, the repetition is transference, impulsion to remember (Freud 2012, 151). Repeatedly bringing one back to the same situation, the traumatic event returns against one's wish. Anna Whitehead claims that "trauma does not lie in the possession of the individual, to be recounted at will, but rather acts as a haunting or possessive influence which not only insistently and intrusively returns but is, moreover, experienced for the first time only in its belated repetition" (5). The traumatic event returns against will after a period of delay. It is not experienced as it occurs, actually for the first time it is experienced through forgetting. "What returns to haunt the victim [...] is not only the reality of the violent event but also the reality of the way that its violence has not yet been fully known" (Caruth 1996, 6).

The event is not assimilated or experienced fully at the time, but only belatedly, in its repeated possession of the one who experiences it. To be traumatized means to be possessed. As Castle puts it, "[t]he mind became a 'world of phantoms' and thinking itself an act of ghost-seeing" (17). Not remembering the past does not make one free of it, it makes one not alone.

The haunting is more persistent when the secret is known to a group of people and yet they do not talk about it, treating it as unspeakable. Then, the trauma resides as much in secrecy as in the event itself, the burden of not telling creates a network of wounds that may even exceed the event itself (Palmer, 118).

An understanding of psychological trauma begins with rediscovery of the past. The past, which keeps surfacing in the present, has to be worked through, relived and reconsidered. Thus, recovery is possible through "cathartic reliving of the traumatic memories" (Herman, 25).

What kind of memories can be traumatic and engender uncanny feeling about domestic space? First of all, the uncanny can be a result of the war trauma. According to Victoria Stewart, "[t]his type of traumatic memory – traumatic both in that it is uncomfortable to experience and brings back an event that was itself uncomfortable – is relevant to the discussion of many Second World War texts" (8). Sara Wasson calls home the nightmarish stage for war preparation and views domestic interiors as sites of war (110). The war transformed daylight interiors into dark, claustrophobic chambers. It was dangerous to move through the cities, and people tended to spend more time indoors. Many of them died under the ruins of their own houses and "the Gothic trope of live burial became literal for those trapped in rubble" (Wasson, 105).

Wasson also offers gendered readings of wartime's disturbing domestic interiors as metaphors for women's lives under patriarchy. During the war women were supposed to fight in the "home front", their role being that of waiting and keeping homes unchanged. The prolonged waiting they endured was oppressive: as Wasson mentions, "[p]assive waiting can be toxic labour, making a home into a space of heterochronous horror. The cruelest entity in these domestic spaces can be time, personified as a ravenous entity" (126).

Wartime homes become carceral heterotopias characterised by hallucinatory presences and bizarre temporalities (Wasson, 107). Their interiors are sites of suffering and temporal confusion, where the past usurps and contaminates the present. But besides the war, other emotionally painful and distressing situations may lay the ground for the uncanny. Not only terrifying events, like violence, can be traumatic, but also such situations as poverty or chaotic life conditions are related to chronic fear and anxiety. In general, the "traumatic disease" may arise from the inability to meet an overpowering emotional experience (Freud 2010).

The experience of loss may also be accompanied by strongly marked signs of subjective suffering and produce the post-traumatic uncanny effect. In Freud, anxiety in children is often the way they express their feeling of the loss of the person they love. Then, every time a person loses somebody or something, he finds himself repeating the same situation in a circle, no matter how distant the first traumatic episode is from others.

Traumatic symptoms have a tendency to become disconnected from their source and to take on a life of their own. "The traumatic event, although real, took place outside the parameters of "normal" reality, such as causality, sequence, place and time" (Felman, 69). Unconscious mental processes are in themselves "timeless". They are not arranged chronologically, and the idea of time cannot be applied to them. And although memory is strongly attached to place, the effect of trauma seems to destroy the very symbolic function of place (Whitehead, 10).

In trauma, there is often a collapsing of time and space, making it hard to achieve distance from the past. Painful memories are relived, with all of the attendant feelings, rather than remembered. Traumatic experiences are typically stored as isolated, non-integrated memories that can easily be stimulated by similar, non-traumatic, sensations. Memory traces are revised and interweave with fresh experiences producing the uncanny effect.

If traumatic experiences are not addressed, understood, and integrated, they can become an overpowering factor in personality development and identity formation. Traumatic events can shatter the construction of the self. Trauma plunges an individual into a state of existential crisis with the sense of alienation persisting.

Nicholas Royle calls this state "the crisis of the proper", when as a result of the uncanny effect one's sense of oneself ("personality", "sexuality", etc.) seems strangely questionable (2003b, 1–2). Royle believes the connection between uncanniness and identity uncertainty is undeniable. The traumatic experience of the person's past contributes to his identity disintegration and makes him see the world and himself differently, feel the danger and unfriendliness of the environment, be haunted by the memories of the past. The person has the feeling of "being after oneself" and undergoing the experience of being double. The trauma narrative can be read not only "as the story of the individual in relation to the events of his own past, but as the story of the way in which one's own trauma is tied up with the trauma of another, the way in which trauma may lead, therefore to the encounter with another" (Caruth 1996, 8).

Uncanny feeling happens only to oneself, within oneself, but it is more like a foreign body within oneself. Analysing the uncanny feeling we detect foreignness in ourselves, in everything which is familiar – desire, memory, sexuality, everyday language and behavior. It dissolves the certainty about the identity of one's self.

The loss of certainty about one's proper self leads to the fragmentation of time and space in the work of fiction. In the case of time, it loses its linearity, becomes retrospective, circular and recurring, whereas space gets unhomely. As Royle puts it "the uncanny can consist in a sense of homeliness uprooted, the revelation of something unhomely at the heart of hearth and home" (2003b, 1). The uncertainty of the self leads to the uncertainty of the world and particularly the domestic space, which is traditionally associated with the stronghold of peace and security, becomes uncertain, strange and obscure.

It is not only temporal and spatial perspectives of the novel that should draw our attention in text analysis. As the uncanny is often centered on the characters' complexes, belief sets, traumata and childhood fears, Kateryna Kühn-Rudenko suggests that the character perspective is indispensable for the analysis of the uncanny effect; the emerging trauma can be depicted in different narrative forms, such as inner speech and free indirect discourse "representing the inner verbal reaction to the quasi-perceived" (179). The characters' speech as such is unwittingly testimonial (Caruth 1995, 24). So, identifying characters' perspectives may help to relate them to their traumatic experiences and trace the origins of the uncanny.

Psychoanalytic reading of modernist fiction offers the possibility of establishing the latent content of the texts through the analysis of the uncanny domestic space. It allows us glimmers of insight into characters' selves and reveals the concealed emotions and transference relationships that have more to do with the personal, misplaced fears and fantasies than the strangeness or instability of the place itself.

Chapter 2. "Homeliness Uprooted":[2] Oppressive Abodes In Elizabeth Bowen's Novel *The House In Paris* And Selected Short Stories

> *A study of Bowen's work should include – even begin with – an exploration of the house that, in one form or another, she repeatedly transformed into literary text.*[3]

1. Domestic Space in Bowen

Modernist fiction is frequently set in in-between spaces, spaces that are occupied only on a transitory basis, that "reveal a fascination with psychological borderlands and relate frequently to such liminal states as the uncanny, the journey, and death" (Drewery, 4). The emphasis these texts place on individual and social liminal states is illustrated in a concern not only with psychological threshold states, but also physical ones, and they centre on liminal places as well as times.

The house is a focal point in many of Elizabeth Bowen's works and very nearly constitutes "the basis of her methodology" (Chafin, iii, vi). She demonstrates an almost obsessive preoccupation with the house in her fiction, treating it as "the core of the world" (Bowen 2008, 39). According to Malcolm Bradbury, Bowen's fiction is "home-based" (145); her novels are "domestic", as R. B. Kershner puts it (68). For Bowen, houses are the foundational element with and around which she structures much of her fictional writing.

However, instead of standing for a site of comfort, safety and stability, the house, in Bowen, appears to be antagonistic to its inhabitants and makes them feel threatened and uncertain of who they really are. In her novels and short stories, Bowen places a strong emphasis on the house as a liminal space which is set in a liminal time. The central action of many of her works takes place at

---

2   A sense of "homeliness uprooted" is described by Nicholas Royle as "the revelation of something unhomely at the heart of hearth and home" (2003b, 1).
3   Vera Kreilkamp, *The Anglo-Irish Novel and the Big House* (New York: Syracuse University Press, 1998), p. 142.

transitional times such as dawn and dusk, childhood and old age, while the dominant liminal images include doors, windows, mirrors, gateways, shorelines, etc.

The atmosphere is an inherent aspect of the house in Bowen. For the author, "the intuitive writer-observer holds in her mind an inner environment, an impressionistic rather than purely geographic space" (Parsons, 30). According to Paul J. J. Pennartz, it manifests itself as a double-sided process: "the atmosphere of a room works on an individual, and conversely an individual projects his or her specific mood on the room" (95). This point of view is also supported by Elke D'hoker: "Bowen's idiosyncratic combination of a variety of figural tropes and narrative strategies results in a strong but highly ambivalent bond between house and character, whereby houses at once illuminate and efface their inhabitants" (267).

Remarkably, the atmosphere in Bowen's novels and short stories is often uncanny. Characters experience the presence of something disturbing and frightening in the house, perceiving the domestic space as strange, sinister and feel entrapped there. As Shafquat Towheed claims, "Bowen's overcharged concern with place, her repeated, insistent and enforced returns in her fiction to the place of an earlier event to reinscribe the validity of a narrated event [...] often through the character's interaction with material objects, verges on the obsessive and the Unheimlich" (113). Her fictional characters are haunted not just by material things or chronological events, but by spaces, "whether occupied, emptied, displaced or imagined; the 'enforced return', the witting or unwitting trajectory of so many of her protagonists, invariably re-engages with a previous spatial experience" (Towheed, 131).

Psychoanalytic theory has provided the most rigorous account of the uncanny as "an unhomely subjective position by evocatively connecting imagery of home to the description of the subject" (Connon, 53). It offers a number of views on the house in relation to the people that occupy it. For instance, according to Freud (1920), the house symbolically represents the female genitals or the female body in general. Freud interprets the fears connected with the house as a transformation of unsatisfied libido. In addition to that, Trigg claims that the orientation and experience of place are fundamentally affective and the totality of experience of place begins and ends with the body of the subject (Trigg, 10).

However, Gaston Bachelard's concept of the house appears to be more appropriate in the interpretation of Bowen's texts. Bachelard regards the house as the representation of both body *and* soul (italics mine – O.L.). He claims that the house stands for the inner, intimate world of a person (Bachelard, 7). The mental image of the house repeats or echoes the inside world of the subject and the image of the house is the imprint of his or her mental state. Thus, if the uncanny is localized within the domestic, one should be looking for its decipherment in the individual experience of the people who inhabit the house.

The homes of Bowen's writing are sites of intimacy (Chafin, vii). Home makes visible to the visitors aspects of its owners' life and actually speaks volumes, while being stubbornly silent. The houses evoked in Bowen's fiction express their inhabitants' personalities and the focaliser's consciousness (D'hoker, 271). "Houses, parks, cafés, and even larger spaces like London and Ireland become problematic containers for subjects. [...] they provide the grounds for intersubjective symbolic identification" (Miller et al 2009, 133). The return to home is often tied up with the "identity quest of the central protagonist and understood as an attempt to return to the self, to know the self and feel at home with oneself" (Connon, 20).

The space in Bowen is "the space of a fleeting anachronicity" (Royle 2011, 122). Bowen's houses have quite uniformly been read as "emblems of the past, as embodiments of a tradition and identity from which her characters are irrevocably severed" (D'hoker, 268). In one of her interviews, Bowen underlined the importance of time within the idea of home:

> The idea of home – that is, the desideratum – now seems also connected with an idea of tempo: inside the four walls there should be *enough time*, temporal if not physical space. Inside the four walls, there should be abatement of the psychological tyranny of the clock. There should be enough time for relationships to develop fruitfully, for impressions and memories to be digested, for feelings and thoughts to connect themselves into a meaning pattern. Modern consciousness, constantly overcharged, requires a resting-place, an unloading-place – that, should not home provide? (Hepburn 2010b, 173).

Through her writing, Bowen infuses her work with the form of the home and "houses serve as foundational institutions within her novels, objects of both geometry and psychology" (Chafin, v). "The habitat, whether large or small, is the container of the essential elements of life; what goes on within four walls has a continuous and creative effect, whether good or bad, on the individual inner being" (Hepburn 2010b, 162).

1.1 Semi-reality of Bowen's Houses

Bowen's novel *The House in Paris* opens with a taxi drive across Paris, from the Gare du Nord, where eleven-year-old Henrietta arrived at the house of Naomi Fisher and her mother. Henrietta is going from London to the south of France in order to stay with her grandmother and, as there is no one to accompany her all the way through, she has to wait for her evening train in the care of Miss Fisher. Coincidentally, there is another child staying at the same house at the same time.

Nine-year-old Leopold has come to Paris from Italy for a few days in order to meet his mother who he has not seen before. However, Leopold is not just a friend's child, he is an illegitimate child of Naomi Fisher's ex-fiancé Max Ebhart and her best friend Karen Michaelis, whose story the reader gets familiar with in the middle of the novel. Eventually, Leopold's mother does not turn up. Instead, her husband Roy Forrestier takes the child, although it remains unclear whether they are going to keep him or send him back to his parents by adoption.

In *The House in Paris,* four houses are represented: Madame Fisher's house (rue Sylvestre Bonnard, Paris), the Michaelis' house (Chester Terrace, London), Naomi's dead aunt's house (Twickenham, England) and Karen's dying aunt's house Mount Iris (Rushbrook, Ireland). The house in Paris is a gloomy and oppressive abode sunk in darkness and silence: "It was exceedingly silent, though you heard in the distance Paris still going on; the height all round would have made it darkish at any hour" (HP, 22). The house is distinguished by its unfriendliness and antagonism; it is uncannily inanimate and alive at the same time, and being inside one inevitably feels under threat:

> The inside of this house – [...] with stuffy red matt paper with stripes so artfully shadowed as to appear bars – was more than simply novel to Henrietta, it was antagonistic, as though it had been invented to put her out. She felt the house was acting, nothing seemed to be natural; objects did not wait to be seen but came crowding in on her, each with what amounted to its aggressive cry (HP, 24).

On the one hand, the Fishers' house resembles a monstrous creature with a spine: "sending vibrations up the spine of the house" (HP, 65); even if it is "asleep", its eyes are still open watching you and radiating a troubling strangeness. On the other hand, it seems to be a sinister prison with "the barlike stripes of the paper" (HP, 57) and the door which shuts behind one "with a triumphant click" (HP, 38). The house in Paris is often compared to a well, an underground, a grave, an island, a labyrinth, in a word, to different kinds of a trap: "Untrodden rocky canyons or virgin forests cannot be more entrapping than the inside of a house, which shows you what life is" (HP, 77).

Furthermore, the house seems small and narrow outside, its hall and stairs are "undraughty" (HP, 24) and it looks like a doll's house. Henrietta thinks "perhaps it is not really so small inside?" (HP, 23) but when she enters it, the inside appears to be more like a well – very deep and dark, almost fathomless: "The room [...] looked on to a courtyard like a well between walls" (26). Henrietta sees many windows from the outside but when she comes into the house there are hardly any there and even the air "darken[s] her lungs with every breath she [takes]" (HP, 49–50).

According to Emily Ridge, the presentation the Fishers' abode as "miniature, like a doll's house" (HP, 22) with "doll's-house furniture" (HP, 26) as well as the depiction of Paris as a "cardboard city" (HP, 19) is meant to convey a sense of semi-substance, semi-reality in which the house exists (Ridge, 116). Indeed, its strangeness and unnatural atmosphere are repeatedly emphasized in the text: the house is called "uncommon" (HP, 50), it is filled with "fumes of insanity" (HP, 58) and the word "mad" is repeated several times in regard to the inhabitants or visitors of the house (HP, 60). Henrietta is surprised to hear a doorbell – "[o]ne forgets that such things go on in Paris too" (HP, 64). Finally, unlike other street or city names used in the novel, Rue Sylvestre Bonnard, where the Fishers' house is situated, is fictional and alludes to Anatole France's novel, which will be discussed further down in this chapter.

The visual image of the house and its surroundings also contribute to the atmosphere of semi-reality: "Unbright light stuck between the flanks of the houses, making their inequality odder still" (HP, 22). The city in *The House in Paris* appears to be an uncanny zone of liminality – familiar and foreign at the same time. The atmosphere is intensified by darkness, silence and emptiness: "dark greasy February morning", "a sinister hour and place" (HP, 17), "a street with so little animation" (HP, 224), etc. The city looks like under a spell, there are almost no people there, it is empty: "shutters were unwakingly shut. In fact, it was early for people to be about - there were no shops, nothing to get to work. But it would not really have surprised Henrietta if no one had ever walked down that street again. […] At each end, the street bent out of sight: it was exceedingly quiet" (HP, 22).

Moreover, some of the objects, for instance mirrors (or other objects with reflective surface), may also contribute to the sense of semi-reality. The episodes with mirrors are often described with the words: "false ease", "imitating", "unnatural" which can suggest false world some characters inhabit or the imitation of living. Therefore, one may conclude that the house in Paris is not supposed to stand for a real place, but rather a place in one's memory or imagination. It is ghostly, full of memories of the past: "The fatal house in Paris still so possessed her that nothing was real that happened outside that" (HP, 186).

Another house depicted in the novel, the Michaelis's house, called Chester Terrace, is also uncanny. It is a "bleak" place where it feels cold even when the streets are glaring hot and where the shadow of clouds makes rooms "darken uneasily" (HP, 95, 98). "The sea of trees" in the park does not look "too smiling" (HP, 127), on the contrary, it casts "an unnatural reflection" (HP, 172), so that "the silk shadows and darkish glow" of the rooms make the house appear "desertedly dark" (HP, 168–169).

The house seems strange, firstly, because it is often depicted and imagined as a living creature; for instance, the construction of the house is often compared to the body which has a skeleton: "news travel downstairs through the bones of a house" (HP, 131). Secondly, the uncanny atmosphere is caused by the aura of secretiveness that hangs over the house: "Sun on the hall floor, steps upstairs in the house had this same deadly intention not to know. [...] To the studio, in the streets, this careful horror pursued her" (HP, 173). The house seems to be the container and the keeper of a horrible secret that it struggles to conceal from the world, turning the inhabitants of the house into its hostages: "This was like being a dog in a house in which they are packing up quietly, or a sick man from whom it is kept that he is going to die. [...] the house with its fixed eye was impelling Karen" (HP, 172–173).

Chester Terrace is also compared to a "shell" (HP, 174), but its calm, although "intoxicating" (HP, 163), is pretended and its safety is the safety of a well-guarded prison. Therefore, it is not surprising that Karen starts wishing to run away, to escape this "'domestic' site of moral decay", to use Melanie Williams's terms (96). The fact that she cannot share her secret with anybody in the house, that there is no space for a sincere talk and for trust there shows how impaired the Michaelis's family is. This kind of impairment can often be found in Bowen's texts; as John Coates notes, Bowen is the master of "defamiliarizing English upper-middle class household scenes" (293).

Mount Iris is another "disturbing repose" presented in the novel, "an unstrange place [that] was never to lose for Karen a troubling strangeness" (HP, 75–76). The house being situated in Ireland makes it seem insecure and settling there pointless for Aunt Violet's English relatives; life in a house in Ireland is compared to life on a raft. The rooms filled with "unsunny sea daylight" look empty but "not so much empty as at a sacred standstill" (HP, 77). The peace of Mount Iris is "fatalistic" (HP, 82).

The estate is also compared to a doll's house: "From the harbor, Rushbrook looks like a steep show of doll's houses" (HP, 75). Like the Fishers' house, Mount Iris serves as a frame for the past events, for memories: "Ghastly black staring photographs of the ruins of Montebello hung at Mount Iris outside the bathroom door; downstairs was a photograph of the house as it used to be, in winter, a grey facade of light-reflecting windows, flanked each side by groves of skeleton trees" (HP, 75). The inhabitants of the house are acutely conscious of time: each room has a number of small clocks, kept going by Uncle Bill, which fill the rooms with the vibration of a metallic titter. Nevertheless, "all the ticking clocks d[o] little to time [t]here" (HP, 81); the house is rather placed outside of time. Like the house in Paris, Mount Iris is a point of intersection of the past (the photos of the old house), the present and the future (the anticipation of Aunt Violet's death).

Most of the houses depicted in the novels belong to women who are dying or who are dead. The house in Paris is owned by Mme Fisher, who is dying. Irish Aunt Violet is dying, too. But most of all, one can feel the contrast of life and death in the description of the place where Karen, Naomi and Max went together. The house in Twickenham presents a kind of antihome. After Naomi's aunt's death her house is offered for sale – at the moment it's nobody's house, a foreign space, transient, in-between the owners, empty: "the aunt's house was hollow, completely dead" with a "bare drawing-room" (HP, 104), it was an "empty house", dusty, with unmown lawn (HP, 115). It is "a place that's hardly a place at all" because the house belongs to somebody dead (HP, 111). The motif of death, loneliness and emptiness is linked to the house. Moreover, it is also the place where Karen and Max meet again after five years of separation. Now they are both engaged, but not to each other. In Twickenham, it is the very meeting that triggers the series of events leading among other things to Max's tragic death.

The objects in the house are often personified and reflect the characters' states and feelings. "Whether as a game, or in deadly earnest [...] the objects of the phenomenal world are granted the capacity to transfer their substance into humans and [...] the reverse" (Rose, 78). In the house in Paris, "the furniture sat so queerly on the floor" (HP, 188). Henrietta hears the aggressive but numb cry of the furniture when she first enters the house. It has been waiting for someone to listen to its story, it is full of memories of the events that happened in the house or to the people who lived there. "Objects that cannot protest but seem likely to suffer" fill Aunt Violet's house (HP, 88). But it is Karen who really suffers, trapped in everydayness and feeling herself being passed like an object from one house to the other (as a result of the future marriage). Colonel Bent suffers too, as he knows about his wife's illness and imminent death.

Finally, the hotel in Hythe completes the list of houses depicted in *The House in Paris*. The "inescapable barred square on the ceiling over the bed" and the "barred light" (HP, 151–152) again refer the reader to the image of a prison. The house is very quiet – "a stone silence going nowhere" (HP, 155) and extremely dark, "built in between the hill and the tight street", with "unlit floor" and "a dark arch"; (HP, 150), the mantelpiece and the wardrobe with its mirror, "darker than the dark walls" (HP, 151).

The houses and hotels Bowen's characters stay at are distinguished by their sinister darkness or shadow. The action often takes place in the dark time of the day or in the dusk, at "a sinister hour" as it is said in the novel (HP, 17). The houses in Paris,

London, the hotel in Hythe are all dark: "dark greasy February morning" (HP, 17), "inside darkness", "the hand [...] in the shadows" (HP, 46), a smile "as deep as darkness and as dazzling as light" (HP, 47). There is already no sun or there is no sun yet: "unsunny muslin blind" (HP, 30), "weak sun" (HP, 66), "the sun [...] never quite shone" (HP, 71). Grey shades are also often used, e.g. grey dust, windows with "dust-grey shutters" (HP, 22), yellow and grey papers, "grey marble mantelpiece with an iron shutter" (HP, 26), "grey swinging silence" (HP, 27), "elm-grey autumn park" (HP, 60) and others. The artificial light may be used, but the light source is always scant, e.g. "that flat clear light in which you think of the past" (HP, 72).

Light is traditionally linked with goodness, life, knowledge, and hope, whereas darkness is linked with evil, death, ignorance, oblivion and despair (Ferber, 112–113). Bowen calls light "sinister energy" (HP, 26). In her novel, the lack of light is connected with a mystery, taboo and dread, even something demoniacal; daunting loneliness is evoked by the light in the falling dark. The power of the chiaroscuro as well as the animation of objects and the pointed unreality of the interior, intensify the atmosphere of uncanniness felt in Bowen's houses.

Clearly, space and especially domestic space receive particular attention of the author of the novel. Bowen uses a wide spectre of techniques in order to create an atmosphere of ambiguity or semi-reality in the places her characters inhabit. The house in Paris and other houses of the novel appear to be uncannily familiar and foreign at the same time and their antagonism towards the characters proves to be the sign of an internal crisis. The house in Bowen's novel is a house turned upside down, an antihome, an embodiment of homeliness uprooted – it is not the place of integration but of disintegration.

1.2 Time and Narration: The Uncanny Return

Time is one of major components in Bowen's novels; according to the writer, it has "the same value as story and character" (1962, 135). But it is not historical time that is important. In *The House in Paris*, there are no references to the year when the action takes place. Dates are almost never mentioned in the novel, one can only come across names of days or months.[4] The track of time is measured not by days or years but by moments.

Unlike traditional narration where time moves in a progressive linear sequence, the modernist novel *The House in Paris* shows rather complex temporal relations. Time in Bowen's novel is narrowed to a single day with numerous

---

4   Except for the scheduled date of Karen and Ray's wedding, which eventually takes place on another day.

digressions: recollections, past experiences embedded in and reemerging into the present. From the very beginning, the names of the three sections ("The Present", "The Past" and "The Present") suggest that the events are not arranged in chronological order. The text is constructed according to a circular narrative structure, the novel having begun in the present and coming back to it. In the first section the action takes place on a February day, Thursday, from the early morning when it is still dark till about half past one in the afternoon; the second section is concerned with the events that happened about ten years before that day; in the third section the action returns to the present Thursday and lasts from about half past one to about half past six in the evening.

"The Present" sections of the novel are closely connected to the events of the past while "The Past" section gives the explanation of the present events. Miss Fisher's care for Leopold is accounted for by her relationship with his father, who she might have married ("…tender feeling for Leopold, which your tie in the past with his unfortunate father will always renew", HP, 41). The pain Miss Fisher feels remembering the events of many years ago makes Henrietta think that the past is not over in that house (HP, 50). It seems to her as small and narrow as a well and at the moments of higher tension (first coming into the house, the episode in Mme Fisher's room and the fragment about the note from Leopold's mother) the house looks and sounds tiny as if not only time but space was being compressed.

The time point is marked in the text as "today": "Today was to do much to disintegrate Henrietta's character" (HP, 25). The deictic *today* does not only position the discourse in time but also reflects the perspective of the character in free indirect discourse. As a signal of subjectivity it marks the events as shown from different characters' point of view. Within the novel one can identify the stream of thoughts of Henrietta, Leopold, Karen and Naomi in different fragments of it. Focalisation is veering, to use Nicholas Royle's terms (2011, 20). Royle suggests that there is never only one voice, one point of view or one narrative perspective, at any one time, in a literary work: where we think we have a transcription of a character's thoughts or feelings, the writing (even if it is a third-person narrative) shows us that the point of view is divided, shared, doubled or multiple (2011, 20). Moreover, in literature, there will always also be the voice or the point of view of the dead (2011, 21). Thus, people in Bowen's texts are often constituted by thoughts, their own thoughts and the thoughts of others.

In *The House in Paris*, Bowen depicts the shifting nature of the modern subject (Magot, 127) reflected against and identified by a temporal background. As Bowen herself states, "We need not seek subject; subject is found by Time" (Hepburn 2010b, 152). The present of the novel is haunted by the ghosts of the past, the recollections continually emerging in the frame of the novel's today. In one of her interviews, Bowen claimed that "today" is the outcome of our past: "when we feel this, no moment seems disconnected, no single sensation seems accidental. How can we consider Today unmeaning when we look back at all that went to formulate it, and us?" (Hepburn 2010b, 152). Bowen's view on subject and time is confirmed by Lacan's statement on retroaction: "In the psyche, present events affect past events, since the past exists in psyche only as a set of memories which are constantly being reworked and reinterpreted in the light of present experience. 'History' of the subject is not simply a real sequence of past events, but the present synthesis of the past. "It is the past historicised in the present" (Lacan 1988, 12).

1.2.1 The Epiphanic "Now"

The first references to the past appear at the beginning of the first section when Henrietta has been handed over to Miss Fisher at the Gare du Nord and they are travelling together to the house. Crossing the city in a taxi they see the streets that "seemed to unreel past again and again" (HP, 17). The windows with strong grilles, solid doors and shutters bring back the times of wars and bloodsheds. The streets are "charged with meaning" that is with their own history, but seem "to lead nowhere" (HP, 22). These references to the past of the city anticipate the remembrance of the protagonists' past. The city and the house are a frame, a stage where a play is acted ("the house was acting, nothing seemed to be natural", HP, 22, 24) and also the present day is a frame for the story that happened many years ago.

The title implies a certain kind of stasis; the house is situated in Paris and thus focuses readers' attention on the specific place where the action will occur. However the house represents a place of transit, an outgoing point from where the "leaps" in time and space are made. The single day the children are spending in Paris brings forth associations and memories related to the Paris of ten years ago, and the reader is recurrently brought back to the events that happened there in the past ("that year in Paris", "those Paris days", "as in Paris", "the Paris past"). However, in addition to flashbacks, foreshadowing also recurs: the story is not only taken back in time but there are also glimpses into what will happen later on in the story: the Fishers' being well-off (HP, 23); Aunt Violet's death and what will happen to the house after she dies (HP, 74, 77); the idea of Leopold that comes to Karen before she realises she is pregnant (HP, 151).

Within the notion of the uncanny Petra Eckhard speaks about "fragmentation of place, time, and self" (17). A similar idea can be found in Nicholas Royle's work, where he describes the uncanny in terms of the "crisis of the proper (2003b, 2). The metaphor of the kaleidoscope used in the text of the novel conceptualizes the relation between time and consciousness. "Feeling like a kaleidoscope often and quickly shaken, she [Henrietta] badly wanted some place in which not to think" (HP, 54). Fragments of the present events, memories of the past and anticipation of the future make up various patterns like small pieces of glass in the tube. Different events, certain people, certain thoughts and images that can be more or less significant at different times tumble in and out of consciousness and induce a transformation of their world view.

Characters' self-reflexive revelatory moments are inherent in Bowen's early writing. For instance, Henrietta's reflections on herself are triggered by observing a croissant dipped into coffee (an allusion to Marcel Proust's episode of the madeleine with its series of perceptional remembrances). The surprise and indignation provoked by Miss Fisher's table manners make her think about her own character ("If I am Henrietta, than what is Henrietta?", HP, 25–26, 50) and of its being made up of prejudices and axioms ("You could not be a someone without disliking things ...", HP, 25–26). On the other hand, Leopold's self-reflection is closely connected with his quest for the past. According to Lena Steveker, personal memory plays an important role in the process of individual identity formation; the self-observation of the protagonists in the retrospective memory process leads to intrasubjective understanding of themselves (4). The lack of this memory and the impossibility of placing oneself against the past may then induce a crisis of identity and engender the uncanny feeling.

Remarkably, the relation between the present and the past in Bowen's novel has much in common with the principle of memory described by Victoria Stewart, which is "conceived not as a movement from the present into the past but as the emergence of the past into the present. ... this past is more real than 'reality' itself" (Stewart, 164). Modernist fiction assimilated much of Bergsonian theory of duration, which presupposes that the flow does not just move in one direction, but each moment contains all the time. The past, the present and the future interpenetrate, resulting in a time-filled moment, a moment of being (Gillies, 126). Memory does not belong solely to the past but it is thought in terms of duration, the reinvoked images appear "here" and "now" and the retrieval of the past is important for the understanding of the present.

When Leopold sees Henrietta for the first time, he recalls spontaneously the memory image of a girl whirling a hoop he has seen in an old lithograph. The hoop as a time entity without a terminus has no beginning or end. This image suggests that time is felt as motion and the text is structured around significant moments connecting present and past experiences. Further in the text we read again: "he saw in her eyes the elm-grey autumn park where the little girl in the lithograph bowled her hoop. Instantly, she became part of his mother's English life" (HP, 60). Thus, the image from the past caused a moment of illumination experienced by Leopold.

The freezing of the time effect is created at the beginning of the section by an immobilization of the objects and the people, a passivity compared to that on the operating table. First there is the exceeding agitation and anxiety of Miss Fisher, the "aggressiveness" of the objects in the house. It is opposed to the quietness of the streets and Henrietta's cold reserve. Finally, everything is immobilized in the salon except the clock's pendulum with its hypnotic disc, which "set the beat of her thoughts till they were not thoughts" (HP, 27).

This state of half-hypnosis and half-sleep coincides with the transfer from third-person to first-person narration:

> Steps crossed the ceiling and stopped somewhere: was Miss Fisher standing by her sick mother's bed? She can't be dying, she wants to know about me. The stern dying go on out without looking back; sleepers go out a short way, never not hearing the vibrations of Paris, a sea-like stirring, horns, echoes indoors, electric bells making stars in the grey swinging silence that never perfectly settles in volutions of streets and empty courts of stone (HP, 27).

The pronoun "me" refers to Henrietta, and her thoughts about Miss Fisher's dying mother are carried on with the flux of associations, sight and sound images of going outside the house, hovering over the city. The past re-emerging in the present also often results in a pause in narration. For instance, when the action is interrupted by a series of remembrances about Henrietta's family (sister, grandmother and father), time seems to stop as after the long description of her family relations it is still twenty-five past ten by the house clock. So, less than a minute has passed.

It is worth mentioning that the change from third-person description to free indirect or direct thought often takes place at the epiphanic moment. When Leopold has read the letters of his mother by adoption and of Mrs. Arbuthnot, he suddenly realizes that he can't go back to Italy and live with the Grant Moody family, he will go to England with his mother. He feels himself a plasticine figure, a person who has been living a fake life: "He saw himself tricked into living. Then I will not, he thought. If he could have been re-embodied, at that moment a black wind would have rushed through the Villa Fioretta, wrenching the shutters off and tearing the pictures down, or an earthquake cracked the floors, or the olivey hill above the villa erupted, showering hot choking ash. Let them develop themselves. I will not go back there ..." (HP, 45). The image of the destruction created by a nine-year-old boy's imagination represents Leopold's indirect thoughts. Although the third-person *he* is used to describe the scene, the final *I* signals the episode being shown through Leopold's consciousness. Thus, memory and subjectivity stand together in Elizabeth Bowen's novel. Remembrances that cause an epiphany in the present come from and through the consciousness of a character and present his or her personal memory, their subjective world.

This sudden realization of the fact that Leopold will stay with his mother, without apparent cause or convincing argument, fully fits in the notion of epiphany given by Sandra H. Johnson. She calls it an "encircled moment of extreme consciousness" and stresses the close connection between illumination and intuition (Johnson, 19). The fragment of a dialogue between Leopold and Henrietta is a good illustration to her view: "'But how do you *know* you're going to England?' 'I know'" (HP, 61). Epiphany can't be learnt but only experienced, witnessed. The verbalization of this moment is realized by special techniques, such as "abrupt transitions and disjointed images" (Johnson, 13). It emerges from the past but affects the protagonists' life, actions and feelings in the present.

To conclude, in *The House in Paris*, the relation of the past and present is reciprocal: "the past not only creates and defines the present for these characters, but also the present creates and defines the past" (Kenney, 48). In her early novel, Bowen extensively uses epiphanic writing in order to allow the reader to peer into the characters' consciousness to see the root of their identity crisis and the uncanniness they feel: "She was interested in the surface of life and in the cracks in the surface of life, and in the terror, passion or pain that is revealed when the cracks open, always irreparably. It can be a remark that does it [...]. It can be sudden winds and chills outside, or sudden draughts and gusts indoors. It can be something indefinitely minor" (Glendinning, 30).

Time is represented as a duration, a flow with no beginning and no end, interconnection of the present, the past and also the future. Memory doesn't send us back to the past but is constantly present in everyday life; memory is duration itself. The text of the novel is constructed as a series of epiphanic moments, "Nows", spontaneous recalls of memory images which appear in the present. They are the means of presenting the events but mostly of depicting the characters' perceptions, peering into their consciousness, showing their attempts at self understanding.

1.2.2 In Search of the Lost Time

The houses of the novel are haunted and their inhabitants are possessed by images of their past. The houses are filled not only with objects and people but also with memories. The time and space relations of the novel are strongly interrelated and evoke Proust's category of felt time: the past can be hidden in material objects, or rather in the sensations these objects produce. "Sometimes objects are enchanting not because they posit an alternative world, but because they encapsulate elements of the known world" (Hepburn 2010a, 34). Marcel Proust initiated a new form of temporality which presupposes memory's dependence on the senses; each object tells a story and these stories accumulate spatially in the interior. As in Proust, in Bowen, time is psychic time, what is important is the coherence between time and space and the strategy of "delving deep down into ourselves, in regaining the time of our inner lives" (Kristeva, 6). The objects from the house in Paris and other houses are called upon to remind of the unresolved past which has to be fully known and assimilated.

Many scholars including Sigmund Freud (1997), Nicholas Royle, Dylan Trigg, Paulina Palmer, Sara Wasson and others agree that space regarded as uncanny is a result of traumatic experiences of the past which have been repressed but return to invade the present. Cathy Caruth claims that "to be traumatized is precisely to be possessed by an image or event" (1995, 4–5). It usually involves time disruption with the past surfacing in the present, especially the past which has not been worked through. According to Allan E. Austin, "all of the Bowen's novels are structured between two traumatic emotional events: the first discloses the reality of life; the second, the reality of love" (22–23). Karen feels trapped in the everydayness and predictability of married life and makes an attempt to escape, which ends with a failure as her lover kills himself. Now, after abandoning her illegitimate son, whatever she does in her life the idea of Leopold being in the world does not let her move on with her life. Even after many years the woman remains in the power of her memories: "But we never are alone, while you're dreading him. It is you who remember" (HP, 217). "Unable to reconcile the contradictory parts of her life, or to eliminate either of them, Karen is unhappily suspended between them in a state of paralysis" (Kenney, 49).

On the other hand, Leopold is traumatized by the realization of his orphanhood. He fails to find the reason why he was abandoned by his real parents and, on his mother's not coming to meet him, he feels twice deceived and deserted. The motif of orphanhood is also emphasized by the name of the street where the Fishers' house is situated. Sylvestre Bonnard, the protagonist of Anatole France's novel *The Crime of Sylvestre Bonnard*, in which the action also takes place in

Paris, helps an orphan girl, the granddaughter of his love of the youth, and protects her from her tutors. He abducts Jeanne from the boarding school of Mademoiselle Prefere, where she is badly treated and takes care of her as his own granddaughter. The motifs of orphanhood and exile are quite frequent and can be found in Bowen's other novels such as *The Death of the Heart*, *The Last September* or *To the North*.

According to Abigail Palko, Karen's whole story presented in "The Past" is filtered through Leopold's consciousness (100). Palko speaks about the biologically inflected psychic split that pregnancy and motherhood can produce in women. She claims that "fictional attempts to narratively capture Bowen's 'the you inside you' are heightened by explorations of the 'you-not-you' that pregnancy creates" (Palko, 91), and that is why Leopold may be the cipher through which Bowen asks us to "read" Karen (Palko, 98). Without doubt, one of the climactic moments of the novel is the night of Leopold's conception. In this episode, Bowen uses the stream of consciousness technique with third-person narration being interlaced with first- and second-person narration (Karen addresses Leopold before he is actually born). Fragmentary, kaleidoscopic writing represents the flow of Karen's thoughts and through numerous memory images the epiphanic moment reveals the meaning and the purpose of the characters' present.

The night of Leopold's conception is the time of "concentrated" uncanniness. Karen and Max meet in Hythe, a port town in the south of England. As Bowen describes it in her essay, it is "a mysterious and important place where present and past mix, one of the 'semi-dead' towns, content to live on their past" ("The House", 57). In the hotel where they stay, Karen and Max get room number 9, which may be an allusion to the nine circles of hell in Dante's *Divine Comedy* or inverted number 6 with its eschatological spirit. Even nature seems to be against the protagonists: the cloudy sky, the rain that "veiled darkening houses and trees make Karen feel they are alone and cut off" (HP, 151). The sun and daylight of their previous dates are opposed to "lamp-invaded darkness" and "frightening luminous watches" light (HP, 151). There was always sun till that day, but on the day of their last meeting there is rain, which "in summer seems a kind of disaster" (HP, 149).

Bowen uses elements of the supernatural in order to heighten or intensify the horror latent in the situation already conceived in naturalistic terms (Brooke, 19). *The House in Paris* is a novel "riddled with apocalyptic metaphors and knotted, tormented sentences, a novel written, it often seems, in a mood of controlled hysteria" (DiBattista, 222). Kenney calls the pattern of life in the novel "neurotically repetitive" (Kenney, 53). This effect is achieved among others by the skillful manipulations of time in the narration. Time can be dangerously speeded up or torturously slowed down, e. g "the week got speed up and went triumphantly over her like a train" (HP, 173). The watches are frightening too, their ticking sounds like heart beating and the clock strike "signals" the hour of death.

Time and space uncanniness causes agitated conditions in the protagonists expressed by the words "anxiety" (HP, 185), "agitation" (HP, 121), "nervous" (HP, 128), "excited state" (HP, 20), "a nervous manner" (HP, 27), "warningly" (HP, 24). It is deepened by marked silence ("exceedingly quiet", "exceedingly silent", HP, 22, "violent calm", HP, 52); fear ("the frightening cardboard city", HP, 19, "dread of Leopold", HP, 32, "frozenly mortified", HP, 35, etc.) and the feeling of the approaching end ("catastrophe", HP, 124, "fatal", HP, 181, "final", HP, 35, "disaster", HP, 149, "tomb", HP, 203, "terrible accident", HP, 196, "misfortune", "death", "dig graves", "dead", HP, 66, "agonized", HP, 207, "crisis", HP, 185, "the world shrank", HP, 69).

Karen has a feeling that the eye of time never stops watching them. The final striking of the clock, the faceless couples they meet on the way to the hotel, the suddenly stopped sound of the piano and the unsalted sea air create a sense of ending and suggest the inescapability and irrevocability of what is going to happen. The dark of the night, the terrifying fingered chestnut leaves and the barred ceiling announce the end. But the weather turmoil anticipates another kind of disaster, that is a child born out of wedlock. He is supposed to be a "poison", an "enemy" that will ruin Karen's and Max's lives (HP, 154, 155). On the night in Hythe, Karen thinks it would be the hour of her death to see everyone know about Max and her, about the child. The weight of being herself falls on her "like a clock striking" (HP, 152).

The child to be born is called an enemy but in fact it is time that is meant: "I should see the hour in the child" (HP, 153). Time proves to be a foreign thing, an enemy to be faced with (remarkably, Mme Fisher is called "an enemy worse than time", HP, 138). Inescapable ordinariness, recurrence, circularity and routine – these are the enemies of the protagonists. "This seemed to have to be, when nothing had ever had to be, so I thought it would be all. It looked like the end". […] If a child were going to be born, there would still be something that had to be. Tonight would be more then than hours and that lamp" (HP, 153)

The child appears to be the only way to take a moment out of the ordinary time flow. The novel's major theme of time and duration, the time-filled moment containing the past, the present and the future is embedded in the child's birth. He is not the end but the mark and the purpose, the hope and the meaning: "He would be the mark our hands did not leave on the grass" or "I could bear us both lying tired and cast-off if it were for him, if we were his purpose" (HP, 153–154). The past life would not be meaningless and absurd for Karen if there was a child in the future. The retrieval of this fragment vividly shows how memory becomes a part of the present, explains it and merges with it.

Thereby, the uncanny in Bowen's novel at first sight suggesting and creating the suspense of a disaster actually implies the "crisis of proper"[5] and the reconsideration of the life and self by the protagonists. Remembering in Bowen's novel has an inward-looking, self-reflexive character and is a means by which protagonists seek their identity. The reemerging of Karen and Max's past in the present is meant to answer Leopold's question of "Why am I? What made me be?" (HP, 67). Timothy D. Adams claims that "the search of identity in *The House in Paris* becomes an exercise in memory, designed to show Leopold in the act of creating his sense of self by simultaneously inventing and remembering the past" (Adams, 50). As for Karen, her return to normal life and retrieving happiness is impossible without the acknowledgement and acceptance of her past.

Most of characters seem to be trapped in their memories or in the memories of other people, and only Henrietta witnesses the house at the moment of being when the past, the present and the future merge together. The house in Paris represents a kind of a frame, a heterotopian portal into other spaces and times, into characters' memories. It embodies a foreign space which is uncannily familiar, striking with its frightening unnaturalness. Thus, the house, in Bowen, appears to be a crossroad, a place of the intersection of people's lives, hopes and expectations, the past and the future, the real and the imaginary.

2. Resisting Domesticization:
The Uncanny House and Marriage

The last part of this chapter is devoted to the discussion of Bowen's uncanny house from the perspective of gender. In order to do that, first, it is worth giving a short overview of woman's role at that period. The early twentieth century was the time of great changes in the sphere of gender relations. The revolutionary climate that reigned then welcomed many new freedoms for women. Their rights and status greatly improved: they were allowed to vote and were recognized as equal to men. Women could attend colleges and do the jobs that only men used to do. Their lifestyle changed as well: they began to smoke in public, wear more daring clothes and cut their hair short.

Nevertheless, the women's rights movement affected some women more than others. In spite of many breakthroughs during the 1920s and 1930s, the free

---

5   Nicholas Royle's term previously discussed in Chapter I.

lifestyle was enjoyed mostly by young, single women, whereas conditions for married women were nearly as restricting as ever. For all the changes in status, it was still generally accepted that woman's place is in the home. It was unusual for a married woman to be employed and the majority of married women worked inside their homes as housewives taking care of their husbands, children and keeping the house.

John R. Gillis calls the period between 1850 and 1950 "the era of mandatory marriage" (229). The compulsion to marry was evident in the early twentieth century. First of all, the pressure to marry had a numerical character: because of the war there were more single women of marriageable age than men. But that was not the only reason. A marriage certificate served as a way to increase the woman's social status. Marriage stood for home and home was necessary for social and material well-being. Nevertheless, the ideal of companionship was rarely achieved in married life (Gillis 1985, 233). Most found their relations with family and friends far more personally satisfying than those with their spouses.

Ina Zweiniger-Bargielowska claims that twentieth century British women embodied Englishness as "domestic and familial life, and the notions of the rooted and stable – belonging, attachment and settlement – that this suggested" (303). But what stability and settlement would marriage ensure for women? The role of woman in the family was generally that of a dependent wife and mother. Gillis calls it "domesticization of the female" (Gillis, 245), especially living in the cities. As they did not work they stayed at home "yoked to their families in subordinate roles" (245).

In fact, twentieth century women inherited much from the Victorian Age. Thus, the main task of woman was to serve man and family. She was "traditionally relegated to the private sphere and entrapped in the patriarchal ideology of domesticity" (Palmer, 109). Woman was the product of the system which oppressed her with home as the centre of "domestic slavery" (Millet, 131). Being inescapably tied to their homes by their families and domestic chores women longed for escape from the so-called doll's house (Holdsworth). The role of an "item of domestic comfort" (Craig, 69) was oppressive for women and could cause different sorts of disturbances connected with domestic space.

In Bowen's fiction, the relationships between men and women fail since women's subjectivity "proves to be incompatible with their gendered identity" (Hinrichs, 4). According to Crowell, the novels of Elizabeth Bowen and other female writers of that period tell about women who reject preordained roles in life (Crowell, 207). Bowen depicts female characters in their unconscious attempt to resist domesticization, they are New Women who "saw the rejection of the past as a radical gesture, one consequence of which was to separate them from the domestic role to which they have been traditionally assigned" (Doan, 96). Therefore, the dark images of the house may as well be the result of their failure. The traumatic losses they go through in their lives come back to them in the form of the uncanny feeling with the house becoming haunted and fear inspiring.

The women in Bowen are trying to reconcile the present and the past reconsidering the choices made or rather imposed. Undoubtedly, the most important choices they make concern marriage. For instance, Karen decides to marry Roy Forrestier, although she does not love him, in full knowledge that this union will help her keep her social status. She inhabits the world where "a woman's real life only begins with marriage, girlhood amounts to no more than a privileged looking on" (HP, 69) and, like other young girls, she has to learn to see love socially. Thus, intimacy and affection, normally central to the ideology of the domestic sphere, is displaced by a social contract. Besides, as Karen assumes, to marry would mean "to keep up the fiction of being the hub of things" (HP, 77).

Karen does what she thinks is right but very soon her certainty about the rightness of her choice begins to dissolve. Like many of Bowen's women, she becomes entrapped by the decision that she has made (Hepburn 2010a, 59). Karen feels imprisoned in everydayness, evenness, "unconscious sereneness behind their living": "her parents saw little reason to renew their ideas", and "were even" (HP, 70), while she was "settled" and knew "what's coming" (HP, 93). She reconsiders her future marriage with Roy and wants to change her life, to break away from the continuity and predictability. She does not want to find herself in a routine life like her brother after his marriage: "This was the world she sometimes wished to escape from but, through her marriage, meant to inhabit still" (HP, 71). Without doubt, the quiet of Karen's home oppressed her.

Karen hates the calmness and passivity and she desperately wants to throw it off by breaking the engagement so promising with the respected man of her class and diving into a secret love affair with the financially unstable French-English-Jew Max. However, her unconscious attempt to escape is not a success, and with Max's death and their child abandoned Karen becomes haunted by the past and seems to be forever the hostage of her memory. The death of Max constituting a traumatic experience of loss for Karen keeps her in the state of time-and-space ambiguity and results in disorienting uncertainty about her self. Moreover, the marriage that follows cements her role of the domestic woman, a subordinate wife entrapped in her "doll's house".

Similar motifs can also be found in Bowen's short fiction. In her short story "The Needlecase", a child born out of wedlock is also placed in the centre of an intriguing plot. The story tells about a Miss Fox, a bleak ageless woman with an "expressionless" face and a "secretive" mouth coming to an upper-middle class family to sew for a week (CS, 455). One of the sons of the family, Frank, arrives home at the same time. Another one, the eldest and the most loved by everyone, Arthur, is expected to come soon with his new girlfriend. The two daughters, Angela and Toddy stay home, bored with its routine and waiting for something to happen.

The house Miss Fox arrives at does not look cheery at all: "The front of the house loomed over them, massive and dark and cold: it was the kind of house that easily looks shut up, and, when shut up, looks derelict. [...] As it was, it was like a disheartened edition of Mansfield Park. The country around it was far too empty and flat" (CS, 454–455). Its darkness is compared to the darkness of a well, and the house itself assumes the features of a living creature: "They saved light everywhere, you had to grope up the stairs, for this well of a house drank money" (CS, 456). To crown it all, the house is "horribly cold", "like ice" (CS, 457), and the stove is either unlit or "a thin fire rather uncertainly flap[s]" (CS, 455).

Miss Fox is received at the house both as a rescue (the ladies' clothes must be mended before the opening of the season), as a curiosity (there is not much going on around), but also as a disturbing presence (her look inspires sublime fear and she is compared to a witch). Her arrival seems to bring more darkness and cold to the already gloomy estate. The way she looks at Toddy is very odd, she looks "as though she were a ghost, as though it were terror and pleasure to see her face" (CS, 456). That is why Toddy feels frightened to be alone with Miss Fox, "at the top of this dark, echoing house" (CS, 456). Gradually, the atmosphere in it is becoming more and more intense, the clouds grow blacker and the whole landscape looks "anxious and taut" (CS, 458). The whistling sound of the wind outside, the house creaking and straining like a ship (CS, 458) or growing silent like a tomb (CS, 459) create the atmosphere of an impending disaster.

Finally, it is revealed that Miss Fox's "odd, reminiscent look" (CS, 456) she casts on Toddy is accounted for by Toddy's startling similarity to her brother Arthur, who turns out to be the father of Miss Fox's illegitimate son. When Frank and Angela peep into the sewing-woman's needlecase, they suddenly see an image that makes them feel shocked and uncanny: "She and Frank both stared at the photograph of the child. They saw, as Toddy had seen, its curls and its collar. Like Arthur's collar and curls in old photographs downstairs. And between the collar and curls, Arthur's face stared back at the uncle and aunt" (CS, 460).

The ambiguous situation Miss Fox finds herself in working in the house of her illegitimate son's father produces an uncanny effect and turns the house into a sinister tomb-like abode. Surrounded by numerous reminders of her "fall" (Arthur's photos hanging on the walls, his brother and sisters looking so like him), Miss Fox experiences a crisis that makes her look like an "immobile shadow", a "sculpture" or a "jointed image" (CS, 455, 458, 453). The story she tells Angela about a dummy damaged by Arthur when he was fooling around with his friends at the house Miss Fox used to work at is actually the story of the damage perpetrated to Miss Fox herself, making her social status, as an unmarried mother, forever low and embarrassing.

While "Bowen's daughters", like those from "The Needlecase", "typically experience the house as safe but suffocating and restricting", to use D'hoker's terms, "the enthusiastic attempts at homemaking of Bowen's housewives do not deliver the promised self-realisation but only emptiness and despair" (D'hoker, 283). For instance, in her short story "Story Scene", Rene Osten, after a few years of marriage, feels entrapped in her husband's house and in their marriage. Her role as a wife comes down to keeping the house nice and being there when her husband needs her, like his favourite pipe he always likes to find "at his elbow" (BOS, 240). Len Osten seems to treat his wife as a piece of furniture, as a part of the house. He likes her quiet ways and feels comfortable with her, as with the rest of familiar things he is used to in the house: "Her compliance (whatever she thought) with his way of life, and her dependence, made her satisfy him" (BOS, 242).

In despair and desolation, Rene starts an affair with Len's best friend Alec but her husband still does not notice. The day she decides to announce her departure Rene tidies all up in the house, changing the usual order of things to finally make Len realise. Her plan works and Len does feel disturbed: "'Oh, you did notice?' 'It hit me in the eye.' 'Things have to do that,' she said, 'or you never notice at all.' [...] 'When you don't notice and don't notice,' she said, 'you sometimes make me feel I shall go mad'" (BOS, 242). However, it appears impossible for the couple to save their marriage and Len remains alone in his house, which now seems unnatural and not quite real.

According to D'hoker, "[h]ouse and husband provide women with identity, a life, but one which is of necessity lonely, monotonous and ultimately destructive" (284). In this short story, like in many others, one can explore Bowen's critique of the domestic ideology and observe how she uncovers the often harsh reality of domestic life for women. She places emphasis on the house as a site of loneliness and oppression: "Especially Bowen's women characters, tied as they are to the house by the domestic ideology that governs their lives, experience house and home as inherently oppressive. The sense of self that the house construes for them turns out to be limiting and lonely; and their devotion to house and home renders them ghost-like" (D'hoker, 287).

In another short story, "Making Arrangements", one can come across a similar motif of adultery and the wife's flight from her husband's house. Hewson Blair is not able to realise why his wife Margery abandoned him. She seems to have had everything – a big house, a nice room of her own, expensive clothes, dancing parties, etc., so, for her husband, Margery's leaving looks like mere madness, and he compares it with committing a suicide. At the same time, his calmness and pragmatism after his wife's leaving is striking, he eats well ("he knew the importance of this", CS, 173), follows his daily routine and makes arrangements about the housekeeping: "He had never seen very much of Margery, his wheels went round without her; all this, if one could regard it rationally, came down to a few readjustments in one's ménage and a slight social awkwardness which one would soon outgrow" (CS, 176).

Apart from not seeing much of his wife, Hewson did not feel the necessity to listen to her either, so now he is not even sure who is the man Margery cheated him with: "he was not interested in these people, the information went in at one ear and out at the other" (CS, 170). With his characteristic rationality, he assumed that the home he had provided for her and the nice things inside should have been enough to make Margery happy, that "this sense of being cognate parts of a whole should suffice for both of them" (CS, 174). The only time when he expresses the feeling of sorrow and anger is when he receives a letter from Margery asking to send her the trunk with her clothes and finishes with tearing them into pieces. After all, he thinks that "[t]hese [dresses] were all his, his like the room and the house" and very likely like Margery herself (CS, 179).

Finally, the short story "The Return" is one of Bowen's texts that emphasize the oppressive role that home stood for for married women at the beginning of the twentieth century. Mrs. Tottenham and her husband arrive back home after a few weeks absence. They do not seem to notice the gloom and hostility of the house the way Lydia, Mrs. Tottenham's companion does. She treats the house as a human being and perceives the return of its owners as a brutal violation of its peace and silence, as an invasion: "During her six weeks of solitude the house had grown very human to Lydia. She felt now as if it were drawing itself together into a nervous rigor, as a man draws himself together in suffering irritation at the entrance of a fussy wife. […] 'Oh, you unhappy house,' thought Lydia. 'They have broken into your silence and given you nothing in return.'" (CS, 28).

From Lydia's perspective, everything inside and outside the house looks desolate and gloomy: "the distorted trees loom dark and sullen", the air is "heavy with decay" (CS, 29), the hall is "dusky" (CS, 28) and the rooms are "restive and disturbed" (CS, 30). In fact, the desolation and disturbance of the house stand for the crisis of Lydia's self: "She was at odds with herself again, at odds with her surroundings. [...] 'I was such friends with myself when they left us together; we were so harmonious and at ease with each other, me and myself and the house. Now we are afraid and angry with each other again.'" (CS, 29).

Lydia despises Mrs. Tottenham and her husband, she feels repulsion towards them, even wants them to die and at the same time finds the thought appalling and hates herself for having it. It is evident that Mr. and Mrs. Tottenham neither love nor hate each other, their relationship is quite impersonal (CS, 29). But in addition to that, Lydia discovers that Mrs. Tottenham used to have a lover and now, after receiving a letter from him, is considering whether to meet him again or not. She finds her employers shallow and snobbish, hypocritical and deceitful and thus not deserving to own or inhabit the house.

However, Lydia's attitude suddenly changes when she realizes how lonely and unhappy can be the life of a woman after marriage. Shut up in that big cold house, almost twice as young as her husband, Mrs. Tottenham had no way to escape from the everydayness, but through an adulterous love affair: "'Because it *was* wrong. It's this awful *rightness* that's killing me. My husband's been a bad man, too, but here we both are, smirking and grinning at each other, just to keep hold of something we neither of us want'" (CS, 34). At this turning point, all Lydia's fears and grudges gave way to sympathy and compassion and the house became "vibrant with humanity", "as though a child had been born" (CS, 34).

All in all, in spite of all social change that occurred in England at the beginning of the twentieth century, the institution of marriage remained quite unchanged. It was still widely assumed that women's place is at home and they had little chance of evading their predestined role. Expected to put their husband's life, career and success before all, women were not treated as full-scale individuals. After a girl married, her identity almost ceased to exist and she was treated as a mere extension of the household surroundings. That is why Bowen's explorations of women's struggles for selfhood are inseparable from her recurring depictions of domestic spaces. Being entrapped in the world where "everything is arranged upon a plan different from their own" (Kent, 149), women, in Bowen, see the house both as home and as a place of their oppression: "Her heroines both flee from and seek houses that function as symbols of a psychic shelter that defines and threatens them" (Kreilkamp 1998, 142). The ambiguity of domestic space and its disintegrative nature create the atmosphere of uncanniness and bring the image of the house in the foreground of Bowen's prose.

Chapter 3. "Suffering from Reminiscences": Memory and Trauma in Elizabeth Bowen's Novel *The Death of the Heart* and Selected Short Stories

> "I just asked about the day I was born".
> "Well, the one thing leads to the other. It all has to come back".[6]

1. The Uncanny Aftereffect

Memory has found a prominent place in the works devoted to twentieth-century literature and especially modernist fiction. It has been conceptualized as a "storehouse", a "container", intrinsically linked to identity and viewed as a temporal phenomenon (Antze, Lambek, xi). The importance memory assumes in Bowen's fiction is connected with the placement of trauma in the centre of her concerns. In Bowen, memory often carries a burden of the past and her characters possess a victimized identity.

According to Dylan Trigg, "the subject that survives trauma does so less through the fortitude of subjectivity and more as the uncanny aftereffect of an event" (237). The deferment of the trauma's work upon the subject establishes a radical split in time and opens a portal between the past and the present. The result of its opening is becoming possessed by the past impossible to be reconstructed in a conventional narrative: "Instead, the place of trauma vibrates with an indirect language, blocked from interpretation and displacing the certainty of self, memory, and place" (276).

Peculiar to the memory of trauma is shifting the focus from what is important onto what may only seem to be so. When analyzing the space of the novel and trying to establish the origin of its uncanniness, it is vital to take into consideration not only the recent past but also more remote events that may have occurred even in early childhood, as "the traumatic event has a magnetic appeal that pulls a wide constellation of experience (often, an individual's whole life) into its orbit" (Roth, xviii).

---

6   Elizabeth Bowen, *The Death of the Heart* (London: Penguin Books, 1962), p. 80.

This chapter will consider memory as a wound and examine the role it plays in the disintegration of domestic space in Bowen's novel and short stories. It will explore the relation between landscape and character, the disruption of temporal continuity by the symptomatic emergence of the past, homelessness and exile, dream and reality, selfhood and otherness.

1.1 Silence, Darkness and Solitude

The domestic space of the novel is presented as alien and frightening, and the house is distinguished by its sinister darkness, emptiness and the cold. For its inhabitants, it can suddenly lose its familiarity and become unfriendly and uneasy to stay in. The house engenders loneliness, alienation and estrangement. But this uncanniness is subjective and originates in the characters' traumatic experience of the past, namely the loss of family (orphanhood or childlessness) and/or homelessness and exile.

As in most of Bowen's novels, in *The Death of the Heart*, the plot is rather intricate. After her parents have died, 16-year-old Portia arrives in London to live with her half-brother and his wife. With her coming to Windsor Terrace, three of them, Portia, Thomas and Anna Quayne, feel weird with each other, as memories of the past begin to saturate the house and their thoughts. In fact, all of them are linked with the same family story. As a result of his liaison with Irene and Portia to be born, Mr Quayne had to leave his first wife and son, and his house, which he loved so much, and was "sent" abroad. Portia and her parents were merely homeless, they "trailed up and down the cold parts of the Riviera, till he [Mr Quayne] caught a chill and died in a nursing home" (DH[7], 14). Mrs Quayne died shortly after that. In short, Portia's family had lived "with no place in the world and nobody to respect" (DH, 78) and she had grown up "exiled not only from her own country but from normal, cheerful family life" (DH, 15).

According to Freud, the uncanny effect is often produced by silence, darkness and solitude (1986). Without doubt, all of the three components are important, but it seems appropriate to start the discussion from the first two. 2 Windsor Terrace, the London house of the novel, is often compared to an underground, a grave or a web; it looks dark and empty and it engenders fear and loneliness: "the hall was a well of dusk – not a light on yet, either upstairs or down" (DH, 22), "the blackness of windows not yet lit or curtained made the house look hollow inside…" (DH, 12), "a house to which nobody had returned yet, which, through

---

[7] Here and further on in the text DH refers to Bowen's novel *The Death of the Heart*.

the big windows, darkness and silence had naturally stolen in on and begun to inhabit" (DH, 22).

Images of emptiness also abound; they are manifestly present in the landscape (the empty park near Windsor Terrace, Covent Garden that "gave a look of hollow desuetude, as though its desertion would last forever" (DH, 329)). Besides, the word "vacuum" is persistently repeated in the description of some of the characters, for instance, Anna or Eddie, a young man she chose to patronize: "There were times when Anna almost hated Eddie, for she was conscious of the vacuum inside him" (DH, 67) or "Eddie's eyes ran over her [Anna's] doubtful face – the light seemed to concentrate in their brilliant shallows; his pupils showed their pin-points of vacuum." (DH, 70).

Jocelyn Brooke insists on the great importance of landscape or the surrounding in Bowen's works and its close connection with the action in the story (5). In Brooke's opinion, Bowen is the kind of a writer who is primarily interested in the atmosphere and what we "see" in the novel is more important than what we "hear". This view does not seem fully justified, as what we hear or rather do not hear in her texts seems equally important. Bowen's characters spend most of the time in silence, which fills and almost engulfs the house in Bowen: "Portia lay in a sort of coffin of silence… Outside the room there sounded a vacuum of momentarily arrested London traffic" (DH, 85) or "a house … to which, through the big windows, darkness and silence had naturally stolen in and begun to inhabit" (DH, 22). The absence of sound or speech intensifies the sense of anxiety that fills the house and its inhabitants and exposes the unnatural ways of Windsor Terrace.

Hariett S. Chessman seems to be more accurate when she underlines the significant role of silence in Bowen's fiction; she notes the inability of the characters to speak to each other and the atmosphere of incompleteness and secretiveness (70–71). Indeed, the language of the novel continually veers, being "distorted and distorting" (DH, 10) at the same time. There is always something that resists being told and thus revealed: "'What's not said keeps,' she went on. 'And when it's been keeping some time it gets what not many would dare to hear.'" (DH, 80–81). Thus, in Bowen's novel not only the landscape but also language and silence are used to disintegrate personality.

Moreover, as far as the atmosphere is concerned, one should not restrict oneself only to what is seen or what is heard. What is also important is what is felt, namely the cold: cold January days, cold hall and Thomas's study, the cold colourless silhouettes of the Regency buildings, etc. The novel starts with the description of a lake covered with ice, islands in frozen dusk, the sunless sky and people wrapped in warm clothes and hurrying home, away from the winter's harshness. The "empty cold clay silence" of inner dark park is opposed to the inside of the drawing-room with firelight "making cheerful play" (DH, 16).

The word "fireplace", sometimes replaced by its synonyms, becomes a key word of the first section of the novel. Throughout chapter two it is mentioned ten times. It is referred to as "fire", "electric fire", "radiator", "mantelpiece" and also as "hearth". The latter usually appears in the language as a part of the idiom "hearth and home" denoting "family", "home" and associated with "warmth". However, the warm and welcoming impression that Windsor Terrace may make on some of the visitors is only an illusion, and the fire only grins "like a fire in an advertisement" (DH, 92). The warmth of the house is ostensible and, instead of genuine warmth, there exists merely an artificial flame: they have lived "packed close in one house through the winter cold, accepting, not merely choosing each other. [...] They had sat round a painted, not a burning fire, at which you tried in vain to warm your hands..." (DH, 149).

Throughout the novel, Portia's attachment to fireplaces is often emphasized: coming into the house she first of all goes to the radiator to feel the hot vibration of the air and to warm her hands up. At tea, she sits on her stool by the fire with a plate on her knees. Her favourite place in Thomas's study is near the electric fire, down on the hearth-rug ("her stool by the fire" (DH, 27); "a high stool close to the radiator" (DH, 178); "her accustomed place on the stool near the fire" (DH, 253); "[she] faced round once more to the radiator and spread her fingers a few inches above it, so that the hot vibration travelled up between" (DH, 24)). One of the images Portia cherishes in her imagination is poking fire and expecting somebody to come home. However, in real life, she remains numbed by the coldness of Windsor Terrace.

The feeling of cold accompanying the characters may be interpreted as a response of the body to the emotional experience of loneliness and loss; for instance, when Cecil feels hurt by Portia he says he has a chill (DH, 223), and when Mrs. Heccomb perceives "any lack by any one of her senses", it always makes her imagine she feels cold (DH, 138). And, conversely, when Portia goes back in her memories to the last months spent with her mother, there appears an image of broken ice, a momentary thaw. Therefore, the natural warmth in the novel stands for the longing for the warmth of the hearth. The attempt to combat the feeling of not choosing one's company at Windsor Terrace, of being merely "packed together" is likely to have made the house "queasy and cold" (DH, 170); and the motif of a fire that does not give warmth, a painted hearth may express a yearning for the lost home and family.

1.2 Landscape and Character

Bowen's characters, states Brooke, are a part of the landscape, and her main preoccupation is to show "the relationships between the individual and his environment" (8). Again, this opinion seems only partially right, as it is the landscape that appears to be a part of the characters and not vice versa. Bowen's fiction often originates from a particular locale but the settings constitute the medium, through which her characters move, not a background, as Brook claims.

The house and objects are often anthropomorphized: not only is the house presented as a living creature, but the objects seem to possess sentience: "Unnatural living runs in a family, and the furniture knows it, you be sure. Good furniture knows what's what. It knows it's made for a purpose and it respects itself … Oh, furniture like we've got is too much for some that would rather not have the past. If I just had to look at it and have it looking at me, I'd go jumpy, I daresay. But when it's your work it can't do anything to you" (DH, 81). On the other hand, people are often compared to objects: Matchett is "the woman with the big stony apron" (DH, 312), Anna feels "like a tap that won't turn on" (DH, 246); abundant in domestic metaphors the novel often stresses the resemblance between house and human: drawing a shutter over one's nerves (DH, 138) or imagining ideas like chairs being rearranged (DH, 188).

Bill Brown emphasizes modernism's capacity to vivify the physical object world. "The past seems to reside in objects; historical insight seems to be graspable from inside the material record, from the way a genius rei seems to animate objects with the presence of the past" (Brown, 112). Objects are transformed from items of possession into objects which oppose the sense of being-at-home. Like the house, they appear to come to life in a disturbing manner: "To the person out walking that first evening of spring, nothing appears inanimate, nothing not sentient: darkening chimneys, viaducts, villas, glass-and-steel factories, chain stores seem to strike as deep as natural rocks" (DH, 123).

However, the furniture which "remembers" the past is only a personification of people's remembering. It is what Freud calls "suffering from reminiscences", when "symptoms are residues and mnemic symbols of particular (traumatic) experiences" (Freud 1997, 88). Not only do they remember the painful experience of the remote past, but they still cling to them emotionally, unable to get free of their memories.

Every novel by Bowen employs at least two locales to help establish a moral perspective, to show one in the relation to the other. In *The Death of the Heart*, there are two main houses described, that is Windsor Terrace, the Quaynes' house in London, and Waikiki, Mrs. Heccomb's house in Seale-on-Sea on the Kentish coast, where Portia is sent for a month while Thomas and Anna are on holiday in France. The two locales are opposed to each other, making the gloominess and secretiveness of Windsor Terrace even more prominent.

The Quaynes' house is a solid brick building which has an outlook "fit for Buckingham Palace" (DH, 82). The streets outside look dark and the buildings have a feeling of menacing depth. At Windsor Terrace, darkness and silence penetrate into the house through the windows. Even after the spring cleaning, it does not look lighter, it is still sunless and cold, with the dusk in the rooms and the light only penetrating into the house "in a ghostly way" (DH, 230). The house is compared to an underground, "a perfect web" (DH, 98); it is gloomy and even when the sun appears outside, the curtains are drawn not to let the sunny glare in. The house smells weird, too, everything has a "charnel" echo and the furniture is covered with white sheets like corpses, resembling a house after a plague epidemic (DH, 151). When the first fog of the season creeps indoors, Portia notices that her window is "like a brown stone" (DH, 114), and she can hardly see the rest of the room. It does not seem like night, but "like air being ill" (DH, 113).

In contrast, Waikiki is very close to the beach, just inland from the esplanade; it faces the Channel, and the sea outside seems to be an annexe of the room. The house "ha[s] an almost transparent front" and the room "hold[s] a light reflection from the sea" (DH, 133, 134). The firelight is seen in the inside dusk and makes the room look gay from the esplanade; in Portia's room, "the electric light, from its porcelain shade, pour[s] down with a frankness unknown at Windsor Terrace" (DH, 136).

At Windsor Terrace, there always reigns a tomb-like hush as in a library; that makes it impossible for everyone to reduce the emotional strain; on the contrary, oppression keeps hanging in the air. The overwhelming silence may sometimes give way to fading sounds or muted voices: "Behind the doors at Windsor Terrace, they had heard each other's voices, like the continuous murmur inside the whorls of a shell" (DH, 149). The image of a shell in Bachelard's *Poetics of Space* is generally associated with a refuge, a space inhabited by a creature that is half dead, half alive, half stone, half man (109); it expresses the dialectics of what is hidden and what is manifest (111), with metaphorical hiding or withdrawing into one's shell being a sign of the repressed being.

On the other hand, Waikiki is a soundbox, it is always noisy there. It is in Mrs. Heccomb's way to shout rather than talk, and Daphne, her stepdaughter, likes hanging around the house with a wireless. One can hear loud steps, sounds of crashing, kicking, clattering and banging all the time. The noises add life to the house and make Waikiki "the fount of spontaneous life" (DH, 171).

At Windsor Terrace the social life is hardly noticeable. "Callers were unheard of, had been eliminated, they simply did not occur. The Quaynes' home life was as much their private life as though their marriage had been illicit. Their privacy was surrounded by electric fence – friends who did not first telephone did not come" (DH, 87). Apart from a few of Anna's friends, nobody visited them, and when they did, Portia felt alarmed and tacitly watched, whereas at Waikiki "no one watched", "no one seemed to object" (DH, 146). The "secretive" life of Windsor Terrace sits in contrast with the openness of Waikiki where guests are welcome and parties are a usual thing, and where Portia sees how everyone feels. At Waikiki, there are glass doors and cupboards, French windows, and the rooms are full of sunlight; even the sea wall is knee-high, as if the house, the people in it and their feelings were exposed, not hidden. Something "edited" life in the Quaynes' house, "the action of some sort of brake or deterrent", whereas "the uneditedness" of life at Waikiki made for behaviour that was "pushing and frank" (DH, 171).

Among other buildings described there are lodging houses in Seale-on-Sea, the Karachi Hotel where Major Brutt is staying, Portia's school and the places where Portia stayed at with her parents. The empty lodging houses at the sea look very much like after a disaster: the creaking stairs, the ends of torn wallpaper fluttering in the draughts, bedrooms like cells, light which only sneaks along, and the church bells heard from uphill make up an atmosphere of a catastrophe. When Portia and Eddy get inside, they have a feeling of having the way blocked, being pursued by something, being threatened, so naturally they become overwhelmed by fear. The desertion and decay add to the emptiness of the houses and allude to the image of death: Portia sees ghostly outlines of the furniture on the paper, the walls are "mouldly blue like a dead sky", there is "a stale charred smell" coming from the grates, and many flights of the rooms are "a dead end" (DH, 196).

The Karachi Hotel is depicted as a giant filled with vacuity, "nothing so nobly positive as space" (DH, 285). The windows are "nude-looking" and there are "deserts of the walls", inside which there could be no intimate life even when the hotel houses used to be homes (DH, 285). "They were the homes of a class doomed from the start, without natural privilege, without grace. Their builders must have built to enclose fog, which having seeped in never quite goes away. Dyspepsia, uneasy wishes, ostentation, and childblains can, only, have governed the lives of families here." (DH, 285) Everything creaks in the house, one can feel convulsions going through the building; mirrors are dangerous because they "swing you round and hit you one in the eye" (DH, 285). Instead of the light, they emit its unearthly reflections. In the dining-room, with its empty tables, echoing gloom and silence, solitude reigns, too. The whole place is compared to a warren or a labyrinth.

The school Portia goes to in London and the pension in Switzerland where she had lived with her mother before she died constitute another pair of locales opposed to each other. The school is connected with her present life in London with the Quaynes, and the pension refers to the past and often appears in her memories as a paradise lost. The former symbolically represents the "bottom" whereas the latter stands for the "top".

The Swiss pension was situated in a "high-up village" on the crag; it was a wooden house with balconies facing the tall pine forest (DH, 34). The description of the pension is rich in the vocabulary which emphasizes its high-upness: "the heights", "high chalets", "village lights at star level", "up the steep zigzag" (DH, 34), etc. Thus, Portia's life with her parents and its sad ending are associated with the top: "Precarious high-upness had been an element in there life up there, which had been the end of their life together" (DH, 34).

The image of the pension only appears in Portia's thoughts and dreams about the past. The days spent in the pension on the crag were Portia's last happy moments with her family and by revisiting them in her imagination she returns to what has been irretrievably lost. Similarly, in the flashback telling about Anna's childhood and the life with her father, it turns out that she also lived in an "uphill house" (DH, 125). Finally, when Portia stayed at Seale-on-Sea and went to a café with Mrs. Heccomb, she observed that "only outsiders drank their coffee downstairs", the "fashionable" part was upstairs, it was bright and sunny and cheerful there (DH, 155).

On the other hand, Miss Paullie's school room where Portia attends classes is situated at the back of the house, in the annexe, so that to get there girls have to go down the basement door. Built for a billiard-room, the school has no windows, only a doomed skylight often covered with a blind, and the ventilation does not work properly. The place reminds of a cellar or a well and Portia can never concentrate at her classes like other girls, she cannot "keep her thoughts at face-and-table level; they [will] go soaring up through the glass dome" (DH, 53).

According to Lotman, the bottom can be associated with "materiality", everyday affairs and the top with "spirituality" (218). The bottom is everydayness, whereas the top is dreams. The bottom is immobility and, as Lotman puts it, it is "equated not only with mechanical movement, but also with any movement which is totally and ambiguously predetermined. Such movement is perceived as slavery, and lies in opposition to freedom – the possibility of unpredictability" (Lotman, 224). Thus, Miss Paullie's school, as well as Windsor Terrace, being compared to an underground and depicted as a dark, entrapping place lacks spirituality and freedom.

Eddie's home and Eddie himself are also associated with the bottom and the word "down" is often used when talking about him: "how down he had been" (DH, 61), "taken down, let down and finally sent down" (DH, 62), "all jobs [...] turned me down flat" (DH, 68). Other words related to the bottom are also frequent when Eddie is described, for instance, "underground passion" (DH, 62), "an underlying practical view of life" (DH, 66), "the underlying morality of his class" (DH, 278). His "downness" is to a great extent considered to be the result of upbringing in a lower-class home: he had been a child of an "obscure home", his family was "obscure" and they lived in "an obscure province" (DH, 62).

Thus, space symbolism plays a significant role in the novel and tells a lot not only about the houses but also about the characters. In *The Death of the Heart*, space is inseparably connected with the set of oppositions such as top/bottom, darkness/light, fullness/vacuity, cold/warmth, etc. where the boundary becomes an important topological feature of space. Among others, in the opposition inside/outside, there is a strict boundary between the house and the outer world. Windsor Terrace appears to be a particular space, separated from everything else that surrounds it: "She's [Matchett's] not in London, she's in the house" (DH, 102). The world inside the house seems to be isolated like an island and those who find themselves inside become affected by its isolation. Moreover, the relations between the inside and the outside are sometimes disturbed, since the interior of Windsor Terrace may suddenly become a reflection of its exterior and vice versa: the poplars outside the house "stood up like frozen brooms" and the rooms of the house became invaded by the outside winter cold (DH, 14).

Additionally, the importance of boundaries in the novel may be observed in the persistent repetition of the image of a bridge. The opening scene of the first section is set at the footbridge where Anna is having a conversation with her friend St Quentin. Later in this chapter the word "bridge" is mentioned eleven times over fifteen pages and it often appears in the following sections as well. The bridge is the place where Bowen's characters meet, where important conversations take place: Anna and St Quentin, Portia and Eddy, Portia and Thomas choose bridges to talk about significant moments of their lives. Built to join two separate sides of the land, the bridge can suggest an emotional tie between the characters or a lack of it. It can be interpreted as a sign denoting union as well as a desire for it. As J. C. Cirlot points out, in many cultures, the bridge symbolizes a transition from one state to another – of change or a desire for change (33).

On the whole, Bowen's characters are bound to the space they abide and the space of the novel may not be analysed separately from the characters. What is also typical is the characters' extreme consciousness of location; even one and the same place may be perceived differently: "When I came in after buying the stamp I felt still odder than I generally do, and the house was still more like always than usual" (DH, 111); "It is queer to be in a place when someone has gone. It is not two other places, the place that they were there in, and the place that was there before they came. I can't get used to the third place or to staying behind" (DH, 223); "This is a new place this week, this is a place in summer" (DH, 228). According to R. F. Foster, locality is linked to "knowing who you are, and who other people are" (160) and thus landscape is often used to reflect the inner truth about an individual it surrounds. Therefore, the uncanny space in Bowen is employed to present a dissolution of the character's subjectivity.

2. The Burden of Memory

2.1 The Uncanny Reentry of the Past

What creates the uneasy atmosphere at Windsor Terrace and do all the characters share the feeling of the uncanny? Major Brutt's impression of the Windsor Terrace house is a warm and a bright one, where one can get a warm welcome. Mrs. Heccomb describes it as a happy house, extremely hospitable. St Quentin sees firelight making a cheerful play in the drawing-room; in his perspective, the house is far from being cold and gloomy, it is warm, pretty, bright and colourful: "the pretty air-tight room with its drawn aquamarine curtains, scrolled sofa, and half-circle of yellow chairs, silk-shaded lamps cast light into the mirrors and on to Samarkand rugs" (DH, 26–27). Thereafter, the house must be subjectively perceived as uncanny by only some of the characters and, as the study will show, they are the Quayne family.

Without doubt, the house is ghostly; it is full of memories of the past, painful reminiscences haunting its inhabitants. As Bennett and Royle claim, "Bowen's text exploits a kind of ghostly temporality" (1995, 68); in her novels, time is veering, shifting from present to past, constantly changing its direction, turning, twisting, whirling in a circle (Royle 2011). Bowen is master of "ghostliness of the present and of 'death' as the condition of speech and writing" (Royle 2003a, 81). Remarkable is her employment of the image of a man viewed as a big fly in the amber of another man's memory (DH, 45). It gives an eerie intensity to the past and creates an impression that the Quaynes are sealed inside a time-capsule.

The story of Portia's birth is a spectral text within the novel; it has been repeated and retold by different characters: first by Anna, then Matchett, the housekeeper, and finally there is a glimpse into Portia's own memory of her mother. Having found out about the circumstance of her coming to the world, Portia seeks to understand who she is, to know the purpose of her being: "They would forgive me if I were something special. But I don't know what I was meant to be" (DH, 79). This may be the reason why she starts writing her diary, she does it in an attempt to reconcile the past and the present and to transform the broken up, fragmentary and often distorted puzzle of events into a meaningful (and thus sensible) story. As for the rest of the family, they would rather forget the embarrassing episode that occurred seventeen years before, but despite their wish they are not able to do it.

According to Ernst Jentsch, the uncanny effect is produced due to the fact of the breach of social taboo; revealing something hidden from the public eye inevitably makes up a dangerous threat and, especially if the concealed element is sexual in nature and is related to the concept of sin (10–11). Portia is received as a foreign and disruptive presence at Windsor Terrace, as her entry into the life of Thomas and Anna is the "reentry of the past", which to them is "cheap, and vulgar" (Kenney, 54). The idea of Portia as his father's daughter embarrasses Thomas, and he is filled with shame "on behalf of his father, himself and society" (DH, 40). After his father's departure he became convinced that one should detest intimacies and should never be attached to anyone: "He dreaded … to be loved with any great gush of the heart" (DH, 39). In this state of fortification he locked himself up in his study and immersed in solitude. Callers, when they did occur, were received with "galvanized" or even "agonized heartiness" (DH, 88, 96).

On the other hand, Anna, who is an orphan too, cannot have children. She had two miscarriages and after that convinced herself and others that she did not want to be a mother. When Portia comes to live with them, she occupies the room which was supposed to be a nursery and will now remind Anna of her childlessness. Since then, Portia and she have been living with each other with an "opposed heart" (DH, 141).

The repetition of the word "heart" in the text, like "the turned-in heart", "the empty heart", "slackening hearts", "light-heartedly" (DH, 60, 124, 184, 21) and many others, and its strong position in the title of the novel – "the death of the heart" may imply the lack of warm feelings, intimacy in the Quayne family, emphasize the indifference and estrangement between them. Windsor Terrace has "some organic failure in its propriety" (DH, 42), it "makes a smell of feeling" (DH, 105). Yet, it is difficult to agree with Yoriko Kitagawa, who interprets the title of the novel as the loss of the inner world (486). The inner life of the characters is not destroyed, as Kitagawa claims, but only their feelings have become "numb" due to the painful events of the past.

The title of the novel is closely connected with the headings of its parts. The three sections of *The Death of the Heart* entitled "The World", "The Flesh" and "The Devil" refer to the three enemies of the soul, three temptations opposed to the Trinity. The dangers coming from the flesh and the world may be linked with seeking social success and corporeal enjoyments. As for the devil, according to J. D. Bernal, it is human psychology, "our capacities, our desires, our inner confusions [that] are almost impossible to understand or cope with in the present" (Bernal), our inner motives. In other words, the devil may be understood as the unconscious. Thomas's father yielded to the temptation of the flesh and the world having an adulterous relationship with Irene and as a result lost his home and dignity in life. Since then, unconsciously, Thomas has shut himself off the world to avoid the temptation and has not let his feelings out, has not allowed himself to care: "In this airy vivacious house [...] there was [...] no point where feelings could thicken" (DH, 42). Nonetheless, Portia's presence shatters and disrupts the allegedly secure world without sensation constructed by Thomas and Anna, and the painful memories evoked by her arrival influence the characters' perception of home and domestic space.

Better still, the uncanny does not only contribute to the fragmentation of space and time, but according to Royle (2003b), the fragmentation of self, too. When Mr. Quayne started seeing Portia's mother, he was still married to Mrs. Quayne. At that time he began smoking much more and, so that no one could see the cigarette stumps, he buried them in the garden, full of shame he might be caught. His embarrassment and uneasiness grew even greater at those few times when he saw his son after the divorce: "In those sunless hotel rooms, those chilly flats, his father's disintegration, his laugh so anxious or sheepish, his uneasiness with Irene in Thomas's presence" had filled him as well as Thomas with an obscure shame (HD, 40).

Portia's birth is the loss of home for Mr. Quayne, the home which he loved so dearly, loved "like a child" (the phrase repeated several times in the text), the home to which he gave so much of his heart (paving the garden, making a stream, etc). And even after many years Mr. Quayne calls "home" the house he used to live in with his first wife: "almost never came home" (DH, 21), "field-glasses had been sent home to Thomas" (DH, 35). Mr. Quayne's house in England was "his place in the world" and, after losing it and being forced to go abroad, he was never able to find the place he would belong to. He was reluctant to settle anywhere with his new family, since, as Matchett notes, "you don't break a person's nature for nothing" (DH, 78). After leaving the country, Mr. Quayne, Irene and Portia always had back rooms in hotels or dark flats in villas with no view. The way they lived, "with no place in the world and nobody to respect" (DH, 78) was sure to leave its mark on all of them.

Emily Ridge suggests that the emotional poverty, ciphered in the title of the novel, may be seen as the outcome of excessive attachment, from which one must break away (114). Thomas feels the weight of his father's solitary years as well as his own but his solitude is imposed by himself. He thinks his father was safe until he fell in love; that was what ruined him and that is why Thomas never wants to feel for or to be attached to anyone. He assumes love can lead to nothing good in one's life: "'We should detest intimacies', says Thomas, 'and no doubt we should be right'" (DH, 309). He builds a wall between himself and eventual intimacy spending most of his free time alone in his study, silent and gloomy.

Although normally the "landscape of memory is a consolation and a refuge", as Foster points out (153), the consolations of memory may fail one because of personal trauma, it may become "a land inhabited by the waking dead" (153), as remembering can open wounds. Therefore, "the death of the heart" may be understood as a withdrawal into one's self as a result of traumatic experiences, the "numbness" of feelings, which have been partially revived by the evocation of memories.

2.2 Disintegrating Homelessness

Bowen's novels often locate the characters' subjectivity in the experiences of early childhood, bringing to light the effects of parental behavior and identity on their lives. "The destructive impact of history is often registered in Bowen's fictions by the suffering of vulnerable children at the hands of manipulative or absent parental figures" (Kathryn Johnson, 213). One of the central concerns in her novel is the loss of rootedness, producing "deracinated" and "ill-at-ease" characters (Coates, 293).

Portia's childhood was fractured by numerous dislocations, lack of stability in her family's living and the shadow of shame that accompanied them. The places they stayed at were mostly empty, deserted for the out-of-season time. They rarely heard or saw people, they mainly saw cows there, and if they heard somebody talking, it would be in German. On the whole, there was no place they belonged to, as they lived like refugees.

As a result of the secluded way of life abroad, Portia is not used to civilization. Having lived in hotels Portia got accustomed to people always coming and going, and now she does not know what it is to socialize. Portia does not talk much to people and when she does she seldom feels that people ask what they really want to know. Portia admits that when she and her parents lived in France they often did not talk. They did not have friends either because, as Portia has put it, they travelled rather too much. Moreover, she is not used to studying. Portia did not go to school, "she had not learnt that one must learn" (DH, 53) and her progress at Miss Paullie's school is very moderate.

Portia instinctively speaks low after dark because she is used to thin walls. And the silence of the park sounds different from country silence, the silence of the shut park is tense and confined. She does not walk in the house but steals over the floor, creeps in unheard, takes her shoes off not to be heard and softly opens the doors. Portia is anxious not to attract people's attention, not to annoy them. She is often unnoticed: Anna does not see her at first when she enters the drawing room, then does not reply to what Portia says as "she had forgotten to listen" (DH, 28). She may be reassured in an empty house where nobody has returned yet, but she feels trapped when more people are there and she has to talk to them. In fact, Portia feels easier outside, she enjoys being in the street better than indoors. She sees her new home life with its puzzles full of dissimulation and "specious mystery" (DH, 60). The cemetery, the strangers in the street and on the bus do not inspire fear in Portia, but the genuine dangers seem to come from the Quaynes' house.

Portia's manners give her away, for instance, she does not know what to do with her bag: she is embarrassed to know that "to carry your bag about with you indoors is a hotel habit" (DH, 55). She is not sure of how she should behave in a public place, a cinema or a restaurant, as she hardly had any experience before. And she is not used to shopping, either; when you live in hotels there is almost nothing to buy: "Having lived in hotels where one's bills wait weekly at the foot of the stairs, and no 'extra' is ever overlooked, she had had it borne in on her that wherever anyone is they are costing somebody something, and that the cost must be met" (DH, 189).

Furthermore, Portia is obsessively attached to objects, "so unnaturally callous" about them that "she treats any hat, for instance, like an old envelope. Nothing that's hers ever seems […] to belong to her" (DH, 9). The explanation that Anna gives is again related to Portia's homelessness in the past: "It may be because they always lived in hotels" (DH, 9). Portia may be so keen on things because they can give a feeling of safety and stability: "Our habitual interactions with objects both bring them to life and impose order on that life; our habits both mark time and allow us to escape from time, as we perform the present in concert with the future and the past. By doing the same thing with the same things you create the illusion of sameness and continuity over and against the facts of disorder and change" (Brown, 64).

Besides, Portia's affinity to the objects may as well be caused by the unconscious attempt to replace love for the family she lost with the love for things. According to Esther Rey Torrijos, objects further reflect the feeling of loss, the perception of the past as lost and irrecoverable paradise (367). Indeed, Portia seems to love the objects in her room and to miss them once in Seale. She seems to care about them as much as one can care about people. "Only in a house where one has learnt to be lonely does one have this solicitude for *things*. One's relation to them, the daily seeing or touching, begins to become love, and to lay one open to pain" (DH, 139).

As a rule, parents are guiding images for their children in thinking about relationships between people; they give models necessary for understanding reality (Brezinka, 125). It is also generally known that socialization primarily occurs during infancy and childhood, and that is also when the child's values are set. The manner in which the child feels and experiences the world, through which he or she understands himself or herself is constructed by the models the parents provided. Portia failed to learn proper social behaviours and became socially awkward, as the models her parents gave her were not normal. Portia grew up in an unnatural environment, or rather environments, as they kept moving from one place to another, living in exile. They led a life isolated from the rest of the world, and Portia's life was fully encapsulated in her father and mother. The isolation from society and, as a result, the lack of social skills contributed to her alienation from the world and perceiving it as hostile.

Portia grew "wild": throughout the novel she is repeatedly compared to an animal, fearful and alarmed, to a wild creature, a bird astray or a rabbit. Anna thinks that "[i]n ways, she's [Portia's] more like an animal" (DH, 8), as she is not really good at family life. When Portia finds out Anna has been in her room when she was out, she is ready to flee: "'Birds know if you have been at their eggs: they desert'", she says (DH, 25). Moreover, Matchett and she have developed a way of communication involving blinks and glances, more suitable for animals than for human beings: "Portia, her hat pushed back from her forehead, stood askance under the light; she and Matchett blinked; there followed one of those pauses in which animals, face to face, appear to communicate" (DH, 23). Finally, when Portia did run away from her half-brother's house and sought shelter at Major Brutt's hotel room, she looked like a cornered prey: "She only looked at him like a wild creature, just old enough to know it must dread humans – as though he had cornered her in this place. Yes, she was terrified here, like a bird astray in a room, a bird already stunned by dashing itself against mirrors and panes" (DH, 287).

As Portia lived in a kind of suspended state, "outside the dominant social order", to use Hanson's terms (60), she acquired a "completely lunatic set of values" (DH, 282). It may be quite adequately illustrated by the fragment from Portia and Daphne's conversation:

> 'Most people get to know their roles – you can see they do. All the other women I've ever known but you, Portia, seem to know what to expect, and that gives me something to go on. [..] You expect every bloody thing to be either right or wrong, and be done with the whole of oneself. For all I know, you may be right. But it's simply intolerable. It makes me feel I'm simply going insane' (DH, 281).

Portia did not learn how to get on with people as there were not many people about apart from her parents, and even they were odd to each other and to the family. When Thomas and they met, "he [Mr. Quayne] did not behave at all like Thomas's father, but like an off-the-map, seedy old family friend who doubts if he has done right in showing up" (DH, 15).

Tina O'Tool rightly notes that Bowen often constructs the central character as an outsider in her social environment, a displaced person, who struggles to understand and assimilate to the dominant culture (236). Portia is introduced into the world of Thomas and Anna as an alien element: she finds herself a complete stranger in London society and it is not surprising that Windsor Terrace seems to her "the court of incomprehensible laws" (DH, 105). She is called "Irene's child", as Irene was untaught herself and often did wrong things when in society, which was itself very seldom. As a result, the symbiotic relationship Portia experienced with her mother, a social outsider, has left her unable to cope with the complexities of upper middle-class life in the Quaynes' house (Ingman, 70).

On top of that, Portia's mother was used to "spying" on people, to watching them living what she thought would be a normal life: living in nice houses, going to restaurants, cinemas or concert halls. Walking down the streets of private hotels after the concert in Southstone, Portia thinks of the music to which her mother and she "had illicitly listened, skulking outside palace hotels abroad" (DH, 185). When Anna and Thomas take Portia to a movie, she feels it is "one of those polished encounters she and Irene spied on when they peeped into a Palace Hotel" (DH, 44). But Portia's habit to watch people does not remain unnoticed by others, for instance, she makes Anna feel uneasy and queer: "I cannot stand being watched. She watches us" (DH, 37). It gives them the feeling of being trapped, of being unsafe: "'You set traps for us. You ruin our free will'" (DH, 250).

As consequence, the uncomfortable feeling of being constantly on display caused by Portia's noticing alienates or even antagonizes everyone around.

Not only does Portia notice and memorize what everyone does but, in particular, what they say. She acts like a recorder rewinding and letting people hear what they said the other day, confronting them with "other themselves" who give them horrors, baffle them, make them feel in the midst of danger: "'she's got us taped. […] it's given me a rather more disagreeable feeling about being alive – or, at least, about being me'" (DH, 304). Thomas Dukes calls Portia one of Bowen's most effective heroines because she recognizes the powerful nature of language (18). That is why it does not seem right to agree with Chessman who claims that "Bowen scatters her novels with female figures who not only resist the narratives they see around them, but who themselves have no language, and who therefore cannot generate other texts" (71). At least in the case of *The Death of the Heart* Chessman appears to be wrong, as, in this novel, language and especially writing is a metaphor for the articulation of subjectivity, since Portia cannot separate her self from what she ever said or wrote and identifies herself with her diary: "my diary's me", she admits to Eddie (DH, 274).

The previous experience of homelessness affected Portia in a way that disintegrated her self and made her feel inferior to others and hostile to the world. When heading towards Mrs. Heccomb's house in a taxi Portia sees high battered rows of houses and asks Mrs. Heccomb who lives there. She gets the answer: "No one, dear; those are only lodging houses" (DH, 133). It demonstrates the feelings people have about lodgers, to whose number Portia's family belonged, they are no one, not really worthy of being spoken about. Moreover, Portia has been repeatedly reminded she is not a lady because of her unsocial behaviour: Eddie is convinced "[t]his all simply goes to show the way [she's] brought up at home" (DH, 204) and Dickie admits he would not marry a girl so unnatural and thus "[un]likely to make a good home" (DH, 167). Therefore, Portia's homelessness has contributed to her psychic incoherence and inability to develop and keep ties with other people.

3. Reality in a Dream or a Dream-like Reality

3.1 The Interpretation of Dreams

One of the sources from which dreams draw material for reproduction is to be found in childhood (Freud 1950). A dream can bring back to the mind remote and forgotten experiences of the earlier time. The traumatized person responds emotionally to the object and events reminiscent of the original trauma, without consciously remembering the trauma itself (Kihlstrom 1997). This can be most remarkably seen in the series of daydreams Portia has. These daydreams, in their majority, reproduce reminiscences of her past and refer to the traumatic experiences of her childhood. Most of Portia's daydreams lead her back into the time when she lived with her parents, in exile, often moving from one place to another, as if running from something or someone like thieves. In her oneiric musings, Portia moves beyond the time and space she inhabits, being carried back to French and Swiss hotels and constantly re-imagining their life there:

> What she did see was the pension on the crag in Switzerland, that had been wrapped in rain the whole afternoon. Swiss summer rain is dark, and makes a tent for the mind. At the foot of the precipice, beyond the paling, the lake made black wounds in the white mist. Precarious high-upness had been an element in their life up there, which had been the end of their life together. [...] They drove down in a fly, down the familiar zigzag, Irene moaning and clutching Portia's hand. Portia could not weep at leaving the village, because her mother was in such pain. But she used to think of it while she waited at the Lucerne clinic, where Irene had the operation and died: she died at six in the evening, which had always been their happiest hour. (DH, 34)

According to Freud, "a happy person never fantasies"; "the motive forces of fantasies are unsatisfied wishes", "a correction of unsatisfying reality" (Freud 1972, 38). With this dream Portia repeats the initial trauma, the death of her parents, of which her daydreams hauntingly remind her. The words "wounds", "weep", "pain" and the image of a rainy dark day which keeps emerging in Portia's memory emphasize the intensity of her loss, and her longing for the "happier" past.

In another daydream, Portia also imagines a rainy day in Switzerland but her memories are interwoven with the events of a more recent past, her life in London and her stay in Seale, and constitute a complicated block of associations revolving around "betrayal":

> At the very sound, on Eddie's lips, of the word, desire to sleep had spread open inside Portia like a fan. She saw reflections of rain on the silver things on the tray. [...] Since the talk with St Quentin, the idea of betrayal had been in her, upon her, sleeping and waking, as might be one's own guilt, making her not confront any face with candour, making her dread Eddie. Being able to shut her eyes while he was in this room with her, to feel impassive marble against her cheek, made her feel in the arms of immunity – the immunity of sleep, of anaesthesia, of endless solitude, the immunity of the journey across Switzerland two days after her mother died. She saw that tree she saw when the train stopped for no reason; she saw in her nerves, equally near and distant, the wet trees out there in the park. She heard the Seale sea, then heard the silent distances of the coast (DH, 256–257).

The feeling of being betrayed, by Anna who had read her diary, by Eddy who had been holding the hand of another girl, and finally by her parents who had died and left her alone in the world, haunted Portia day and night, filled her mind and induced the feeling of being guilty about all the misfortunes that happened to her. Hence, her longing for sleep, for "anaesthesia" and thus for life without memories.

Portia's other daydream is actually closer to a night dream. Normally, daydreams are a blend of memory and imagination, but this one is beyond the history fixed in her memory. What she saw in her dream had never happened and is not fully intelligible or coherent. The manifest content of the dream is as follows: Portia sees a continent in the late sunset. Eddie and she are sitting on the step of a hut, back to the door. She does not know what is in the hut but she feels its darkness. Unearthly level light is streaming in their faces penetrating their dark hearts. The continent rings with silence. They are sitting with their hands hanging down peacefully. Portia feels calmness and sense similarity (DH, 85–86).

Heijnen and Edgar point out that dreams in narratives are always "event-oriented" (223). Moreover, Freud claims that the true meaning of a dream has its starting point in experiences of the previous day (Freud 1997). Thus, it is worth going back to the events of the day before Portia had the dream. She was agitated by two things – a letter she had received from Eddie (a young man Portia starts being attracted to) and a talk she had with the housekeeper Matchett about her parents and her birth. Now, according to the dream interpretation procedure elaborated by Freud, in order to reveal the latent dream-thoughts, one should collect the ideas and associations appearing in connection with each separate element of the dream. The following elements can be singled out: the continent – the sunset – the unearthly eternal light – the darkness (dark hearts and the dark hut) – silence – peacefully hanging hands – calmness and similarity.

The continent is associated with Portia's life in France and Switzerland, exile, travelling, hotels and finally with her parents. The hands hanging down peacefully resemble nothing but the position of dead man's hands and are associated with death. So is the sunset (as the end of the day, the death of the sun); and so are silence and calmness. According to Trigg, darkness tends to refer to that which is beyond representation, nameless, other, traumatic (234). As for the light, it is not enclosed light which filters to the outside because the hut is lighted out-of-doors. While the hut with the light inside stands for the concentration of intimacy in the refuge, as Bachelard points out (37), the dark hut is a negation of this intimacy, a lack of it. However, according to Freud, "ideas which are contraries are by preference expressed in dreams by one and the same element" (1997, 42). So it is likely that both light and dark mean the dark, which again refers us to "death" or "loss".

If we go back to "dark hut" and "dark hearts" (allusion to the title – the death of the heart) we can get "lack/loss of home" and "lack/loss of love". The graphic closeness of the words "heart" and "hearth", which is also repeated in the text, intensifies the connection between heart and home, lack of home and lack of feelings. As Brooke rightly claims, *The Death of the Heart* is a novel about "insensibility, the emotional atrophy" (22–23), but this atrophy originates in the characters' traumatic loss.

The sense of similarity Portia feels towards Eddie may lie in the fact that they are both lonely. As Eddie confessed to her once saying: "I [Eddie] do feel homeless and sad" (DH, 152), and wrote her in his letter: "You and I are two rather alone people" (DH, 54). Moreover, the figure of Eddie in her dream may as well be the projection of her own ego. "When my ego appears in the dream", claims Freud, "the situation in which it is placed tells me that another person is concealing himself, by means of identification, behind the ego. In this case I must be prepared to find that in the interpretation I should transfer something which is connected with this person – the hidden common feature – to myself" (Freud 1950, 213). Portia and Eddie are called "dreadful twins" in the novel (DH, 95), so it may be assumed that her ego is disguised behind the figure of Eddie, once again emphasizing her homelessness and solitude.

According to Bachelard, daydream is more powerful than thought; "[i]t is our unconscious force that crystallizes our remotest memories" (16). Portia's dream proves to be a missed reality, the reality which can only produce itself by repeating itself, repeating the same loss. It is her trauma revisited, an encounter with the real that must take place each time anew.

Portia's reiterated fantasies and dreams are also a way of escapism. As Zvi Giora suggests, re-living the past in dreams and fantasies is a way of avoiding painful remembering (169). Besides, in most hut dreams people hope to live elsewhere, to flee in thought in search of a real refuge (Bachelard, 31). As Portia was deprived of the original warmth and protection of the family house (the places where Portia was raised can hardly be associated with warmth, neither was it a house, but a sequence of rooms, cold villas and flats), in her dreams, she craves for a safe place to be.

The dream is reactive to the emotional concerns of the dreamer; its meaning is typically a wish or a combination of wish and fear (Kramer, 163). One dream may be substituted by another, but the dream thoughts, the motivation for the dream – the trauma of loss – remain unchanged. A dream is not only an experience but also a question one needs to find an answer to: "Dreams tell us what we otherwise could not know. We peep through the bed curtains that box in our mortal four-poster, and we get a momentary glimpse of the hidden future, the past before we were born, or a present unknown to us. In short, we make supernatural connections beyond our ordinary paths in time and space" (Holland, xiii).

3.2 Waking from Reality

Not only do the dreams in Bowen's novel refer us to the real events of the past, but the plausibility of the present is often questioned. According to Paul Ricoeur, dream is a text (Ricoeur after Obeyesekere, 55); it can be viewed and analysed as a narrative. Alternatively, one may well assume that a text can also maintain characteristics of a dream. It can depict a fading picture full of strange juxtapositions or absurd combinations, where the dreamer cannot pinpoint what is real and what is not. After all, as Bowen states in her novel, "To write is always to rave a little" (DH, 10).

Some of the critics have already noticed the surrealist tendencies in Bowen's fiction. For instance, in her article "Elizabeth Bowen, Surrealist", Keri Walsh stresses the writer's exploration of surrealist aesthetics and discloses the movement's techniques she uses in her prose – automatic writing, the "femme-enfant", "convulsive beauty" and shock (128). Also, Eudora Welty once mentioned that "[i]n the Bowen confrontation, we are guided through the kind of dream-construction that fiction is" (194). And although Walsh and Welty were referring to Bowen's later fiction, if one looks closely at *The Death of the Heart*, one will be able to notice the hallucinatory and dream-like nature of this earlier Bowen's novel.

The imagery of a dream begins with the description of winter London, with nature asleep, hypnotised, as if in a trance. Then, later when spring comes and warms up the icy lake bringing life to the city, the evenings still seem "a dreadful hour", when everything "seem[s] not only to exist but to dream" (DH, 123). On the whole, Bowen's text abounds in surrealistic descriptions such as the following one:

> At different moments, they both crossed different bridges over the lake, and saw swans folded, dark white ciphers on the white water, in an immortal dream. They both viewed the Cytherean twisting reaches at the ends of the lake, both looked up and saw pigeons cluttering the transparent trees. They saw crocuses staining the dusk purple or yellow, flames with no power. They heard silence, then horns, cries, an oar on the lake, silence striking again, the thrush fluting so beautifully. Anna kept pausing, then walking quickly past the couples against the railings: walking alone in her elegant black she drew glances; she went to watch the dogs coursing in the empty heart of the park. But Portia almost ran, with her joy in her own charge, like a child bowling a hoop. (DH, 124)

The mysterious cipher of the swans, the strange combination of dark and white, the interchange of silence and sounds contribute to the image of a bizarre landscape from a dream, a dreamscape, forming a different kind of reality, mysterious, ambiguous and strange. Indeed, this technique has proven to be productive throughout the whole novel.

In this dreamlike episode, Anna and Portia are moving across the same space but in opposite directions. They are shown walking as if in retarded motion; the colours they see – purple, yellow, white, the sounds they hear – horns, cries, birds singing, make up a kaleidoscope of sensations that are nearly attacking them with their intensity. But behind the bright colours and the sounds, there is a hollow, a vacuum, an empty space ("the empty heart of the park", "the transparent trees"); even the flames are not real and have "no power". In spite of the insistent pronoun "they", Portia and Anna are walking "alone", separated by the lake, existing in different dreamlike realities. Similarly, a feeling of emptiness is experienced by St Quentin while walking with Anna in the same park: "They had been walking fast, in this dreadful dream, for some time, when he cried loudly: 'These lacunae in people!'" (DH, 251). The closeness of "being beside oneself", claim Andrew Bennett and Nicholas Royle, and an opening onto the "phantasmagoric multiplicity of otherness" is what marks the space called "dream wood", a space which haunts every romantic or social relation (Bennett, Royle, 75–76).

The image of a child bowling a hoop, which appears in the description of the park, is a reference to Bowen's earlier novel *The House in Paris* and the idea of time as duration where the past, the present and the future are all interconnected. In memories, there is always a compromise between reality and fantasy, and the remembered past does not correspond to the real. Memories, like dreams, are symbols of hidden preoccupations (Antze, Lambek, xii). Remarkably, the clock is usually the element that draws a boundary between dreaming and waking life, the past and the present; as a rule, it is the clock striking that signals the transition from one state to the other.

On the whole, practically all the characters feel or at least once felt that their life was a dream. Mr. Quayne "had got knit up with Irene in a sort of a dream wood" not realizing he would have to stay in that wood for ever (DH, 19). The closeness Portia feels to Eddie is that which "one most often feels in a dream"; it is "a closeness to life she had only felt, so far, when she got a smile from a stranger across a bus" (DH, 59–60). In her diary, Portia writes: "This morning Mrs Heccomb did not say anything, as though yesterday had been all my dream" (DH, 222).

For Major Brutt, for instance, the Quaynes' house becomes a dream, an unattainable and unfulfilled wish: "Almost unremitting solitude in his hotel had, since his last visit, made 2 Windsor Terrace the clearing-house for his dreams" (DH, 86). Being a lonely middle-aged man with no job, no friends and very likely no prospects, Major Brutt "already began to attach himself to that warm room [...] – here was the focus of the necessary dream" (DH, 91–92). He even walks like in a dream: "that erect walk of the sleepwalker – his usual walk" (DH, 291).

Furthermore, the description of Thomas's study gives a pervading sense of being under an impenetrable sheath of sleep: "The vibration of London was heard through the shuttered and muffled window [..]; lamplight bound the room in rather unreal circles; the fire threw its hard glow on the rug" (DH, 32). Thomas's room is viewed as if in a dream or in opium inebriation – unreal, distorted, with the sounds muffled "as though one were half deaf" (DH, 32). In his study, Thomas seems to plunge into a state of half-sleep, the state where "one seems to be a creature of one world as much as the other" (States, 17) and where imagined and remembered experiences merge into a kaleidoscopic flux.

Gradually, dreams and sleep start to acquire greater importance than waking life, since, in dreams, people's real wishes and wounds are disclosed. "'I can't see why the idea of sleep should offend you as much as it seems to'", says Eddy to Anna. "It is the natural thing on a rainy spring afternoon, [...] especially in a nice quiet room like this. We ought all to sleep, instead of talking away.'" (DH, 256). Eddy's suggestion that they all should sleep instead of being awake may imply that only dreams may give them the right answers to their questions, tell them the truth about their real selves.

Portia, too, starts feeling that dreams are more real than waking life and that she is being kept "in the haunted outer court of the dream" (DH, 141), in "some bad dream from which she still must not wake" (DH, 298). More and more often she feels herself a dreamer who can't change what is going on around her but only passively observe, witness things happen: "her body looked like some drifting object" (DH, 298); "Lilian gripped Portia's bare arm in a gloved hand: through the kid glove a sedative animal feeling went up to Portia's elbow and made the joint untense. [...] Like the girl who has finished the convulsions of drowning she floated, dead, to the sunny surface again" (DH, 268).

Therefore, the waking life of the characters is often depicted as lacking sense, empty or even deathlike, while the reality, the true meaning is hidden behind the veil of sleep. Dreaming becomes a way to conciliate the past and the present, to peep into the self in order to liberate oneself from the haunting memories.

In conclusion, the domestic space of the novel is presented as foreign, unnatural, frightening and thus uncanny, but its uncanniness originates in the characters' traumatic experience of loss. The monstrosity of the house and the hostility of the objects become a sign of the misplacement of fears and anxieties from the characters' selves into the place they inhabit. Dreaming is what allows the past to come forth, as what is unconscious may appear in a disguised form only, and what is repressed can be expressed only indirectly, in a distorted and displaced manner. Therefore, through interpreting the characters' dreams and fantasies, it is possible to reveal their repressed wishes, fears and traumas and to show how the domestic space of a novel can become a container of memory, a reflection of its inhabitants' personal identity.

4. The Shadowy Other in Bowen's Short Fiction

In many of Bowen's short stories there is an "indiscernible extra", to use Luke Thurston's terms, that intrudes on the relations between self and other (11). Her writing reaches towards a point of otherness lying beyond the surface of belonging.

Bowen's short story "The Apple Tree" opens when Simon Wing's weekend party are coming back to his house after a concert. The guests do not seem very willing to be back home because of its queer atmosphere and "oppressive" comfort (CS, 463). All the way to the Wings' house, Simon's friends Lancelot and Mrs. Bettersley feel alerted because of what is waiting for them inside, so that even the outside environment seems sinister to them: the combination of wind and moonlight is "nerve-racking" (CS, 461), the sky is "eerie cold" and "pale" and the trees are "windshaken" (CS, 462).

Remarkably, the first word with which the story begins is "frightened" (CS, 461); it is repeated many times throughout the text, sometimes being replaced by a more intense "horrified" (CS, 465). Surprisingly, the source of the fear appears to be Mr. Wing's young wife; in spite of her innocent looks, she is the one to be scared of. Although Myra Wing is hardly nineteen and is often referred to as "the child", it is her presence in the house that makes it queer and frightening: "'You think she *is* what's the matter?' 'Obviously there's nothing funny about the *house*.'" (CS, 462) The "mannerless, sexless child, the dim something between a mouse and an Undine, this wraith (…), this cold little shadow across a hearth" (CS, 463), Mrs. Wing seems to be only half human and even her physical presence in the house is questioned by some of the characters.

Almost jokingly, she is compared to a werewolf at the beginning of the story, but as it turns out later she bears much more similarity to the monstrous creature than it might seem at first. By Brian J. Frost's definition, "a werewolf is a man or woman who, either voluntarily or involuntarily, is supernaturally transformed into the shape of a wolf" (2003, 6). The transformation, temporary or permanent, traditionally occurs under the influence of the full moon. However, with the appearance of Jungian theory of "a beast within us all", the phenomenon of werewolf has been viewed also from the standpoint of the role of the personality in dissociation (Otten, xxvii).

After having witnessed the suicide of her classmate Doria, who had hanged herself on an apple tree in the school garden, Myra's nerves were ruined, in part by the horror of what had happened and in part by the feeling of guilt. She started sleepwalking, and every time she was in this half-conscious state, she stood looking fixedly up and pointing at something above her head. This metamorphosis was bloodcurdling and turned the room where she was into a trap, "a cul-de-sac", making even her husband, "a man with the humility of a beast", become helpless and ill (CS, 464). Neither Lancelot, nor Mrs. Bettersley could hide their shock on seeing Mrs. Wing in her transformed state: "horrified, horrifying – of something high up that from the not quite fixity of her gaze seemed unfixed, pendent, perhaps swaying a little" (CS, 465).

The way Myra Wing skipped the concert in the village hall points at her unwillingness to leave the house after dark. And although she seems to be unaware of when this metamorphosis occurred or what brought it about, the insistent repetition of the images of moon and moonlight in the text and the fact that Doria killed herself on a moonlit night suggest that the moon is one of the factors that triggered this horrible change in Mrs. Wing.

Mrs. Wing's night transformations may be the result of dissociation of her personality, revealing the Other within her self. According to Charlotte F. Otten, the Other is identified as "the kind of person who has never been socially assimilated, who feels rejected by the community and even by the family" (Otten, xxviii). Myra, like Doria, was not pretty as a child; an orphan and an outcast at school, she was rejected by other children. So, as soon as she had a chance to make friends with "more successful" children, she left Doria thus subjecting her to loneliness and suffering.

The tragic event of the girl's death was carefully concealed from the public and especially from the other girls; it was treated as if it had never actually happened. The ill-fated tree had been cut down, the school had been closed, but Myra never managed to forget the sight of branches and the dead girl's legs swaying from side to side against the moonlit sky and the sound of apples falling on the ground. Her fixation on the event is to a great extent connected with her feeling guilty of

Doria's death, making her come back to the uncanny moment again and again. However, finally, she gets liberated from her past, in part thanks to talking about it for the first time: "when it's once out it won't hurt any more" (CS, 467).

In the short story "Home for Christmas", Tom Brosset brings his bride Millie to his family home for Christmas. The Brossets' house seems quite hospitable: the silence is enjoyable, Tom's family are kind and smiling. However, from the very first meeting, there arises a weird impression of the whole scene having been rehearsed: everybody seems to play their roles, even Tom. At breakfast, Tom's family keep glancing at each other and carefully picking up words as if trying to hide and to hint at something at the same time. The increasing tension can be felt, although "there seem[s] no physical reason to feel fear" (BOS, 315). Soon, it appears obvious that the last time Tom was at home at Christmas something awful happened that has made the family feel awkward and ashamed. The same events may have become the cause of Tom's "queernesses", "to which their honeymoon [had] accustomed her [Millie]" (BOS, 310, 318) and which aggravated with their arrival in the house.

Tom's agitation and nervousness noticeable on the day of arrival (brisk movements, swerves and mad veering of the car lights on crossing the house gate) increase the next morning when he sees snow outside. While Millie is glad to have a White Christmas, it seems to be disturbing for Tom, who looks out of the window "in a queer, rather caged way" (BOS, 310). This is not the only reference to the house being a cage, for the text is abundant with claustrophobic images: the house is full of passages, cut-off rooms, "perplexing number of doors", some of which are sound-proof, and "the piercing light let in by skylights and windows" (BOS, 315). Although the house is called "homey", its inhabitants walk there "with rather ironly happy steps" (BOS, 312).

When the Brossets talk about anything, they always finish by mentioning the last Christmas with Tom; merely mentioning, as they never really talk about it, only exchange abrupt phrases and send brisk remarks across. Their speech is fragmentary and allusive, and unease is present in all the conversations. Unable to bear the strain, one of Tom's sisters, Wendy, betrays the tragic story of the last Christmas to Millie. It turns out that a few years ago Tom brought a girl, his fiancée, home for Christmas. It was also snowing on that day and they were enjoying themselves playing hide-and-seek in the dark, but the girl got shut up in a chest in the old schoolroom which made her go mad and die. However, Wendy, unlike Olivia, who had let the girl out, was not aware of the fact that it was Tom who had put her in the box because she had changed her mind about marrying him.

The girl's madness and death were such a shock for the family and especially for Tom that he could not get over it. Since then, the rooms in the house have seemed to be "damned by the past" (BOS, 318), full of memories unbearable for him. That is why when Millie urges Tom to show her all the remote corners of the house including the old schoolroom, she nearly gets shut in the same box herself.

> School books and juvenile books in the bookcase gave out, in spite of the heating, a dead smell. Under one window stood a strong deal chest, hasped with iron: it stood the height of a table and was about five foot long. This room had not been decorated for Christmas; you could see that nobody came in here – and from here the snowy landscapes outside the windows looked metallic and threatening. The room seemed to stand in a frightened trance from the light (BOS, 315).

In fact, it is Millie who gets frightened, almost horrified by the room and its atmosphere of death, by Tom's curious smile and the way he kicks the chest offering her to look inside. With the painful memories having been brought up, he loses touch with reality and feels the compulsion to repeat the event of the past, which becomes more real for him.

From the very beginning, the present in the house seems unreal: when Millie wakes up from "a deep, plausible dream", she finds herself in "the unreality of this unknown spare room silently glared into by the snow" (BOS, 309). Also, Tom tends to escape from reality by cocooning himself in an enclosed world of his marriage, where "nobody knows". While sleeping, he is lying like "a papoose", rolled in the bed, and, at one of his "queer" fits, he wraps himself into *Millie's* eiderdown (italics mine – O.L.) unconsciously searching for the feeling of comfort and safety imitating a position in the mother's womb.

Throughout the text, the characters are overwhelmed with a feeling of being watched, followed by something or somebody that does not belong to the real world. Even the snow seems to be a curse: "'I could swear *she* sent the snow'", says Tom (BOS, 312). The snow is a reminder of the last Christmas Tom spent in the old house; with its bright whiteness it stands in contrast to the darkness of the shut chest and the closed nature of the family secret. The snow "glare[s]", "glimmer[s]" and "glitter[s]" in the sun (BOS, 309, 312) and the light it reflects pierces the house. The whiteness of the snow, of the doors, of the mantlepiece and of the ends of the beds intensifies the white reflection frozen on Tom's face. On the whole, the white colour is used in the story to express the fear of the house or rather of the past that is connected with it (e. g. when Millie comes down from the schoolroom, she looks unnaturally white with horror).

By bringing Millie home, Tom is unconsciously trying to repeat the same scenario as with his first fiancée, hoping that this time it will have a happy ending; he expects that it may help liberate him from his painful memories. And although the story ending does not give the reader an explicit answer whether he succeeds or not, as in the previous story, speaking about the past does not only bring relief but often releases the character from its permanent burden.

Another of Bowen's stories, "The Cassowary", is set in a remote and half-empty mansion called Crecy Lodge. The gates of the house are rusty, covered with dust and "open reluctantly" (CS, 314), which indicates that Crecy Lodge is not very popular with visitors. The Lampeters, new tenants of the house, lead a reclusive life and their residence, standing off the road and obscured by the lime trees, seems to be a perfect place of exile.

The house has a peculiar form: it is over-large and asymmetrical, with a minaret in the Gothic style and pointed windows on one side and a long room with a rounded end on the other. The house thus looks a little like a cassowary, a big bird with a long neck and a round body. Cassowaries are known for their hostility to people, and so is Crecy Lodge. It stands gloomily and bleakly inspiring fear to the people in the neighbourhood, with its "darkly cavernous or lividly-shuttered windows" (CS, 314), which had a "black stare" (CS, 320), and "total blackness down the slippery drive" (CS, 318). The darkness and emptiness invade the inside of the house as well, for instance the drawing-room is "blackly dominated by a mantlepiece like a cenotaph" (CS, 315), other rooms are "bare" and even the inhabitants of the house have "a slight air of vacuity" (CS, 314).

The comparison of Crecy Lodge to a cenotaph is especially significant, as it reveals the main point about the house being an "empty tomb", a place of mourning for a man whose fate is obscure. The man is Paul Melland, a medical missionary who went to Central Africa and got missing two years ago. As nobody had heard from him since that time, he was considered dead by most people, but not by the Lampeters. Paul Melland was supposed to marry one of Mrs. Lampeter's daughters, although, at first, it is difficult to tell which one, since Paul has been engaged to Phyllis Lampeter for more than four years, but before he got missing he had changed his mind in favour of Nathalie Lampeter.

The story about the missing missionary might be amusing to their neighbours (Robert Bonner has made his family laugh till they cry by reciting a limerick "I wish I were a cassowary / On the plains of Timbuctoo, / I should eat a Missionary, / Coat and hat and hymn-book too", CS, 318), but, in Crecy Lodge, the anguish caused by Paul's disappearance seem to be all-absorbing. The uncertainty as to whether he is alive or not or whether he will marry Phyllis or not, has made their life unsettled. The two years of waiting added distress to the family and increased alienation between them. Mr. Melland, "taboo but intently vital", was present in every room and in every conversation (CS, 319) and his shadowy presence haunted the lives of both the young girls and their mother.

Finally, in Bowen's story "The Shadowy Third", the main character and the owner of the house is oppressed by the feeling of déjà-vu wherever he goes or whatever he or his new wife do about the house. His wife's ideas concerning the house, the objects around and even the smells remind him of his first wife who died. The baby they are going to have and the furnishing of the nursery make him constantly think of the child from his first marriage who died too. He tries to escape from his memories and get rid of the things his first wife may have liked or used (he takes the clock off the wall, he confiscates his new wife's thimble case which looks the same as the one belonging to his first wife, he wants to buy a new sofa instead of the one *She* used to sit on so often, etc.), but instead of forgetting his life with her, he keenly feels the absence of the objects she bought for the house. For instance, he keeps putting out his hand to sweep aside the portiere as he passes through the archway, although the portiere was removed a long time ago: "Funny how he could never accustom himself to the changes; the house as it *had* been was always in his mind, more present than the house as it *was*" (CS, 78).

However, his obsession with the past of the house is not only caused by the feeling of loss, but also by his pervasive guilt at his first wife's death. As it is gradually uncovered in the text of the story, Martin did not love his first wife, and his indifference may have killed her. In the recalled episodes of their life together, it cannot be unnoticed that he was always annoyed, irritated or angry with her. He never came home by the early train as he does now and often slipped home pretending he had not seen her waiting at the station. The only way his first wife is referred to is "*She*" or "*Anybody*", whereas Martin's second wife is called "little woman" or "Pussy". But despite the fact that his second marriage is happier than the first one, neither Martin nor his new wife feels safe in the house, they are frightened by the idea they took somebody else's happiness, somebody else's life.

Thereby, the ghostly presence of the Other in Bowen's fiction is linked with the characters' traumatic experiences of the past. The unconscious representations of the trauma are encoded and stored in their memory, and these unconscious memories appear in the form of intrusive images and hallucinatory visions:

> To remember can be at times no more than a cold duty, for we remember only in the limited way that is bearable. We observe small rites, but we defend ourselves from the rooms, the scenes, the objects that make for hallucination, that make the senses start up and fasten upon a ghost. We desert those who desert us; we cannot afford to suffer; we must live how we can (DH, 148).

Although forgetting seems to be necessary in order to survive, the inability to completely forget or adequately remember the painful events of the past provoke a dangerous split in the characters' psyche and result in the haunting presence of the Other that they feel.

Chapter 4. The Spectre of the Big House in Elizabeth Bowen's Novel *A World of Love* and Selected Short Stories

> *When I visit other big houses I am struck by some quality that they all have – not so much isolation as mystery. Each house seems to live under its own spell, and that is the spell that falls on the visitor from the moment he passes in at the gates.*[8]

1. The Big House Tradition

The motif of the Big House is pervasive in Irish art and culture, and it is thematically central in Anglo-Irish literature. The Anglo-Irish Big House pattern has shaped the sensibility of many artists and writers and has become the monument of Anglo-Irish society, with its conservative commitment to the idea of property and the pervading aesthetics of decay.

"Big" is a relative concept: the term "Big House" refers to a "country mansion, not always so very big, but typically owned by a Protestant Anglo-Irish family presiding over a substantial agricultural acreage leased out to Catholic tenants who worked the land. As rural centres of political power and wealth in Ireland, most Big Houses occupied property confiscated from native Catholic families in the sixteenth and seventeenth centuries." (Kreilkamp 2006, 60). Later in the eighteenth century, as a result of the introduction of land laws, the Protestant Anglo-Irish dispossessed the Catholic Gaelic Irish of their land and relegated them to a marginal position in society. Interestingly enough, soon members of the Protestant Ascendancy developed an Irish identity and considered themselves Irish, although their "Irishness" was never the same as that of the Catholic Irish (Rauchbauer, 4).

From the very beginning, the Big House has been charged with emotions (Lubbers, 17). In Ireland, Anglo-Irish Big Houses reflected the disparities of class, ethnicity, religion and language, engendering the feeling of foreignness and insecurity among the Anglo-Irish, the ambiguity of their identity. Colonial oppression led to hostility towards the Anglo-Irish; the Catholic Irish disliked Big

---

8   Elizabeth Bowen, "The Big House". *Collected Impressions* (London: Longmans Green, 1950), p. 195.

Houses, regarding them as "monuments of landlordism and oppression" (Bence-Jones, xxiii). The Big House was considered to be a gloomy place because of its Protestant-Puritan ethic (Henn, 214) and the location of identity solely in guilt (McCormack, 366). On the whole, the Big House became a "metaphor for the failure of individuals to understand each other's motives and aspirations" (Donnelly, 137).

Researchers, including Richard Gill (1987), regard the Big House as a symbol of isolation as well as community. Gill claims that the house gives off an air of unreality, and a sense of loss lingers there (Gill, 53–55). The Big House was usually set apart from the village, behind great walls, and was a manifestation of not only physical but also intellectual and spiritual isolation in which the inhabitants had to live (Lubbers, 18–20). The vast lands around it made the impression of loneliness and secretiveness of the place. In Bowen's words, the houses were isolated like "islands" and their isolation was "innate" (*Bowen's Court*, 20).

Elizabeth Bowen herself belonged to the Big House tradition. Coming from an Anglo-Irish Protestant family, she inherited Bowen's Court, a Big House in the south of Ireland. In the seventeenth century, her ancestor Henry Bowen, a colonel in Cromwell's army, was granted large tracts of land at Farahy. Later, third Henry Bowen, started the building of Bowen's Court in county Cork, the works being completed in 1775. The house belonged to the Bowen family till 1959, when Elizabeth had to sell it, as she was no longer able to meet the costs of its maintenance. Its new owner demolished it in 1961.

Unlike Bowen's Court, many Big Houses were burnt during the Anglo-Irish War (1918–1921) and the subsequent civil war (1922–1923), or given up by their owners in the following years. A few of them are left in a good state (e.g. the Goore-Booths' Lissadell), others lie in ruins. Nowadays, the ruined country house is a frequent sight in Ireland. Many houses, if they can no longer be maintained as private houses, end up derelict with their contents dispersed. The Big-House world has become more and more marginalised (Rauchbauer, 10). It is regarded as a "broken world" and is often studied within the postcolonial trauma (11).

1.1 Big House fiction

Big House fiction may be defined as "exploring the interaction of people within the house and sometimes with the community outside" (Rauchbauer, vii). According to Kersti T. Powell, the staple ingredients of Big House fiction are: a dilapidated house, the rise and fall of a gentrified family, irresponsible landlords, and the rise of the peasant class. Vera Kreilkamp claims that the Anglo-Irish Big House tradition suggests common anxieties, insecurities and fears (1998, 12).

The fears of the Anglo-Irish Protestant Ascendancy, growing into obsession or even paranoia, are those of the Irish peasants taking over their house and land, and these fears are usually intertwined with guilt. This is a trend inaugurated by Maria Edgeworth and followed by other Big House writers. However, in Elizabeth Bowen's works, as in the works by Sheridan Le Fanu and Charles Robert Maturin, the threat does not come from the outside but grows from within, from the Protestant family itself (Powell, 115). When the family secrets are too violent or too real to be contained, they "explode the safety net of a secure and familiar-looking Big House structure" (Powell, 116).

A sense of place is central to Big House fiction. The settings – country, region, estate, or house – exist more often as "the troubled sites of negotiation, anxiety, alienation, and loss than as landscapes of evoking home and community" (Kreilkamp 1998, 21–22). The Big House as a setting is possessed of special atmosphere. It is "a house of isolation – rootless, lifeless, empty of feeling" (Gill, 59). And the occupants are victims of their fixations on the past, living there in a kind of emotional limbo. The notion of the Big House is that of being unable to accommodate emotionally those who seek shelter in it (d'Alton, 3). Thus, in fiction, the houses create, obsessively, a sense of insecurity.

As Paul Gilbert points out, the Ireland of Elizabeth Bowen is the Ireland of the Big House (207). She is called a "writer of evocation and atmosphere" (Hartnett, 1), "a gifted fabricator of atmosphere and climate" (Medoff, 74). Born to an Anglo-Irish family, the last owner of Bowen's Court, Elizabeth Bowen had a deep sense of place and atmosphere. The interrelationship between people and places and the value attached by the Irish Ascendancy class to the Big House are traceable throughout her work (Malcolm, 105).

Bowen's writings are coloured by her experience of a Big House, the image she inevitably returns to in her novels and short stories. Her non-fiction work *Bowen's Court* provides a biographical context for the sense of homelessness of her fictional protagonists. The vision of place and history depicted in *Bowen's Court* pervades all of Bowen's fiction, casting the destroyed Big House as a representation of an emotional life gone awry. In her writing, the recurring plot posits a world without security or permanence with protagonists longing for the imagined security of a lost home (Kreilkamp 1998, 141).

Ian D'Alton treats the house in Bowen as an observer, protector and co-conspirator, claiming that it is "on the same side as its inhabitants, all outsiders in this land, frightened rather than frightening" (6). D'Alton sees the houses as much victims as their inhabitants. However, as it will further become apparent, this point of view does not seem justified in the case of Bowen. The house and its inhabitants cannot be aligned; the relations between them are far from these of allies, the houses being antagonistic towards their inhabitants.

The Big House is a haunting setting and evocative symbol. Often hollow, dilapidated, or abandoned, houses are "sites of conflict and, especially for women, potentially destructive, the haunted house being a prime trope" (Malcolm, 105). Elizabeth Bowen "follows Anglo-Irish characters through decline and disintegration" (Weekes 2006, 189); many of them are displaced or dispossessed, searching for a sense of place and identity. In her fiction, the unconscious relation between the inhabitants of the house and their history, the pervasive rootlessness and insecurity are generated by the inherent ambiguities and contradictions of her colonial origins. In her essay "Pictures and Conversations", Bowen writes: "As a novelist, I cannot occupy myself with 'characters', or at any rate central ones, who lack panache, [...] or who have not at least a touch of the ambiguity, the ultimate unaccountability, the enlarging mistiness of personages 'in history'" (128).

Declan Kiberd stresses the observant detachment which is characteristic of Anglo-Irish writing in general and of Bowen's writing in particular. He claims that Big House writers seek to view man as if he were a foreign, non-human, witness of himself (Kiberd, 366). According to Kiberd, Bowen wrote "not so much to record as to invent a self, a self which lived on the hyphen between 'Anglo' and 'Irish'. And she explored the moment when the self peeps out of its cocoon" (368).

The Big House functions both as stage and as symbol. It remains a constantly felt symbolic presence in Bowen's novels and short stories. Without doubt, Bowen's most famous Big House work is her novel *The Last September*. It is one of her early works but also one of the most critically appraised. The novel is set in Ireland during the Irish War of Independence but the main action takes place in Danielstown, the country estate of the English aristocrats, Lady Myra and Sir Richard Nalor. It describes the life of the Ascendancy as artificial, self-involved, the house being an island in the midst of social and political tribulations with the increasingly militant Catholic Irish nationalism.

The Last September articulates the decay of the Anglo-Irish class embodied in the decay and final destruction of the Big House. The life in Danielstown is unnatural, theatrically static and unconcerned, whereas the house assumes the characteristics of a shell separating its inhabitants from the real world and encapsulating them in their everlasting past: "Projecting its inhabitants' psychic lag, Danielstown is a denial and a stasis: captive to an etiolated past, attitudinized, sensuously parochial" (Blodgett, 27).

The Last September is a work of postcolonial literature with its cultural ambiguity and emotional insecurity of the Ascendancy. It represents the Anglo-Irish cultural loss (Wightman, 37) by apportioning both blame and sympathy to the Anglo-Irish (Wells-Lassagne, 459). Remarkably, the Big House becomes a symbol of the Irish colonial past, an anachronism, a foreign object within the body of Ireland.

The image of an Anglo-Irish Big House also appears in Bowen's other novels, such as *The House in Paris*, *The Heat of the Day* and *A World of Love*. It is depicted in her Irish short stories "Her Table Spread", "Summer Night", "The Happy Autumn Fields", "Sunday Afternoon", and "Hand in Glove". Moreover, the Big House motif is also productive in Bowen's short stories which are not necessarily set in Ireland; like a phantom itself, the Big House haunts and pervades most of Bowen's works.

1.2 Big House Short Fiction

Elizabeth Bowen's short stories "Her Table Spread" and "Sunday Afternoon" depict an Irish country house where hosts and their guests are having a party, leading careless conversations and indulging in food, drinks and music. As in *The Last September,* the house is presented as an island, isolated from all that is going on in the world, whether it is the Anglo-Irish Trade War or the Second World War. In "Her Table Spread", the castle is situated on a hill at the estuary. Its windows look out on the river, which reflects its height, and the waters around make the castle look literally like an island. The house is sunk in isolation, "beautifully remote", among the "lonely waters" (CS, 419), and the thick plantation of trees and bushes makes it nearly invisible down from the shore.

In both short stories, there is a guest who comes to the party from London and whose point of view is contrasted to that of the Big House inhabitants. In "Her Table Spread", Miss Cuffe, a young unmarried heiress of the castle, invites Mr. Alban, hoping to win his affection, while Alban does not seem to be attracted to her at all. He has a negative opinion of women and marriage in general and views the idle Anglo-Irish landlady and her entourage as a bunch of madmen: "he had been warned, he had been warned. He had heard they were all mad." (CS, 423)

Mr. Alban's visit coincides with the appearance of an English destroyer which, by the terms of the Treaty, was permitted to anchor in those waters. It is both a stirring event for the country people, who "are coming down from the mountains to see it", and a pivotal moment of the party, immediately arresting everyone's attention: "So this was what they had here, under their trees. Engulfed by their pleasure, from now on he [Alban] disappeared personally." (CS, 419)

In the story, the castle is often shown from the outside, as if it was being watched from a distance. The candles are lit inside, only to be seen from the water, the French windows are open inviting more visitors, possible those from the ship, and everything around the house loses its familiarity and becomes strange in expectation of something to happen: "Outside, day still lingered hopefully. The bushes over the edge of the terrace were like heads – you could have sworn sometimes you saw them mounting, swaying in manly talk. Once, wound up in the rain, a bird whistled, seeming hardly a bird." (CS, 420)

Bowen's detached style, with its description of the house from a certain distance and introducing a foreigner, Alban, in the company of guests, is used to expose the carelessness and futility of the Anglo-Irish lifestyle and to suggest the inevitable degeneration of the class. Valeria Cuffe, the only heiress of the Big House, is said to be "abnormal" and "detained in childhood" (CS, 419). Indeed, her manner cannot be called regular. She runs in and out of the rooms, "races" around the house with a lantern like a savage; she does not speak but "shouts" or "exclaims passionately" and her abrupt and "impulsive" movements at the table make her aunt feel embarrassed (CS, 419, 421). In addition, her overexcitement caused by the presence of the destroyer and the idea of seeing military men results in her taking Mr. Alban for one of the Navy officers who, she naively imagines, will marry her. Actually, the naivety of the young heiress borders on madness.

Like the whole Anglo-Irish class which gradually moves to its inglorious end, Valeria, "childless, in fact unwedded" will end the line of the Big House landlords (CS, 420). Even the English ships, which used to pass the house once or twice a year, will soon disappear, as in 1938 the Anglo-Irish trade agreement is to be signed between Ireland and the United Kingdom, settling the Anglo-Irish Trade War and making the Royal Navy abandon the Irish Treaty Ports (Hachey, 175–176). What will become of the castle then? It will be sold or go to ruin, like many others of the kind. The destroyer thus may be regarded as a sign of the house's impending destruction.

In "Sunday Afternoon", the Big House is regarded as a lost paradise, but also as an illusion or a phantom. Henry Russell comes to the peaceful Irish country house from London to visit his friends one Sunday afternoon. The party has settled on the green lawn in front of the house enjoying the late spring sun and ready to be entertained by the newcomer's stories. The peacefulness and almost pastoralism of the Irish scenery, for Henry, stands in contrast with English wartime London and reminds him of "the aesthetic of living that he had got from them" but which he had "insensibly deserted" (CS, 616).

However, very soon Henry realizes that the ideality of their world has a tinge of artificiality and affectation, that its isolation from the painful present is the result of their inherent desire to stay in the past: "An air of fastidious, stylized melancholy, an air of being secluded behind glass, characterized for Henry these old friends in whose shadow he had grown up" (CS, 616). But the "sweetness" of their life cannot be eternalised. Henry sees that the peacefulness of their abode is illusionary and will not last forever: "She said to Henry sharply: 'But you'll go back, of course?' 'To London? Yes – this is only my holiday. Anyhow, one cannot stay long away.' Immediately he had spoken Henry realized how subtly this offended his old friends. Their position was, he saw, more difficult than his own, and he could not have said a more cruel thing." (CS, 618). Although Henry has lost his apartment in the bombarded London, and everything in the apartment, which is a considerable loss for him, he still thinks that his position is better because he lives in a real world, unlike the Veseys, the Big House owners, whose existence is suspended, up in the air, like a bubble.

Nevertheless, having experienced the loss of home and of all the "beautiful" things he was so much attached to and "wanted to live with" (CS, 619), Henry warns Maria Versey against leaving her home in Ireland. "You will have an identity number, but no identity" – he says (CS, 622). He assures Maria that once she leaves that world of illusion she will never belong to it again: "'You know,' he said, 'when you come away from here, no one will care any more that you are Maria. You will no longer be Maria, as a matter of fact. [..] You are you only inside their spell.'" (CS, 622). In this story, home and identity are presented as a unity, and when a person loses his home, a part of his self is lost as well[9]. In addition to that, there is a close focus on the characters' attachment to their property. The suggestion that Henry might prefer to stay at home and die in bombardment as a result of which his house and furniture were destroyed, emphasizes how strong the Anglo-Irish sense of possession is and how they fail to detach man from his property: "'It was by chance I was out when the place was hit. You may feel – and I honor your point of views – that I should have preferred, at my age, to go into eternity with some pieces of glass and jade and a dozen pictures'" (CS, 619).

Among the uncollected and unpublished short stories by Elizabeth Bowen, there are also a few that use the Big House imagery in spite of being set elsewhere. In "Christmas Games", the story revolves around a sinister English country house. Phyllida Haughton, a 20-year-old Canadian girl, alone in England, is invited to spend Christmas with an English family she has never met

---

9 According to Deborah L. Parsons, the experience of dislocation and loss of self is a recurrent subject of Bowen's war-time writings (Parsons, 27). However, as we have demonstrated it in the previous chapters, the theme extends to her pre-war works as well.

before. From the moment she started her journey from London to the remote village Little Birdover, where the house is situated, everything seems wrong and ill-omened: Phyllida is late for her train and is nearly late for the last bus; the mention of Ravenswood Hall in the conversation with the country people produces "an uneasy blend of constraint, condolence, suspicion" (BOS, 295); the road to the house is gloomy, "stygian" (BOS, 306); and even the objects in the house seem "to stand at alert" (BOS, 299). Mrs. Throcksby, the owner of Ravenswood Hall and an alleged old friend of Phyllida's late aunt, looks like "the Wolf Grandmother" with "something avid in those glittering eyes" (BOS, 30), and all the company (Mrs. Throcksby's two nephews, her invalid uncle and her companion), sitting tensely without uttering a single word, seem to have conceived something monstrous, expecting Phyllida to be a part of it. With the help of Felix, one of the nephews, Phyllida finds out about the family's propensity for witchcraft, and they both escape from the house before the demonic plan is realized. The young couple is sheltered for the night at one of the farmers' houses in the village. In the morning, they find out that the "Christmas games" did go off and ended up in a big fire at Ravenswood: "Ravenswood Hall – who knew quite at what hour? – had burst into flames, to become a blazing furnace long before help arrived. So great had been the heat that it cracked the walls: they fell, leaving nothing, this Christmas morning, but fuming rubble." (BOS, 308).

The story contains an apparent allusion to Poe's "The Fall of House of Usher" and Le Fanu's *Uncle Silas*, demonstrating strong Gothic sensibilities. But what is more, "Christmas Games" manifests its strong connection to the Anglo-Irish Big House tradition. Firstly, it touches upon the matter of postcolonial relations: it is no coincidence that the main character is a representative of another country colonized by the English, Canada. Phyllida's sense of space described in the story may as well apply to the Anglo-Irish. Used to large spaces around her, she feels trapped in overcrowded London, "dazzled by many lights of small shops", "lost in a mirror maze" (BOS, 293), and tries to make up for homesickness with a Christmas Eve at "friends" in a secluded country house. Her not feeling at home in the country instills ambiguity into her sense of identity and puts her in the position of the other, not belonging to the place.

The final burning of Ravenswood Hall may be interpreted as a symbolical rupture of the bonds tying the Anglo-Irish to England and the English. The collapse of the English traditional house may stand for their desire to get rid of the Englishness that is still a part of their selves and distinguishes them from the Gaelic Irish. Thus, a postcolonial reading of the story allows regarding the Gothic element within it as a sign of the Anglo-Irish disturbed identity where its English component is being suppressed by the Irish one.

Another story by Bowen, "The Claimant", although not set in Ireland, can be fully acknowledged as a Big House narrative. An old English couple moves from their city dwelling to the country and settles in a newly-repaired ancient house. Arthur has sold his business and they decide to retreat to a nice quiet place in the West Country where Arthur can go sailing and his wife can cultivate her nice little garden. It seems that they finally are able to fulfil their old dream, but hardly have they set up in their new home when they receive a strange letter, which spells the death of their happy life.

Letters in Bowen's fiction have their sinister power and often bring a twist of the plot. The letter the old couple gets comes from Australia, from the late Mr. Hobart, the previous house owner's nephew, claiming that the house belongs to him under the will and that it has been wrongly disposed of. Whether the young man is an impostor or the lawyers have made a mistake selling the house to the old couple is not revealed, but since that time Arthur and his wife are never to find peace again. They are not able to put the matter out of the mind and feel indignation but at the same time pity for the young man.

The telegraphic style, with short simple sentences, emphasizes the growth of tension between the couple and the place. Here is a passage which describes the letter coming by post: "We'd been in the house three weeks when the letter came. July. It was drowsy weather, dulling over sometimes in the afternoons but again bright throughout those evenings. Time passed itself – how, I need not tell you. I know I had not yet got the curtains up. But what matter? We went to bed before dark." (BOS, 184). The elliptical sentences, sometimes consisting of just one word, make the narrative highly intense and heavy, with each word laid before the reader like a cobble-stone. The remark that they did not pass the time but it passed itself marks the self-governance and inescapability of what is going to happen.

Young Hobart does not give up and sends them another letter stating his intention to come in person in order to "thresh the whole matter out" (BOS, 187). This second letter "read like the work of an angry maniac" (BOS, 187), and on receiving it, the apprehension they feel has changed into fear. Abandoned by lawyers, they feel endangered and despised by the village people – everyone seems to them to be in league with the Hobarts. Very soon they develop a full-blown paranoia: "How they knew that the nephew was coming I could not tell you – but *they* knew all right. We read that in every eye." (BOS, 187)

Their paranoia becomes even stronger when they read a newspaper note about the air crash in which all passengers including P. St. J. Hobart died. In spite of the claim that they "cease[d] to worry", their anxiety, mingled with shame for feeling relieved, make their life in that house impossible. The typical for Bowen "emotional weather" mode, typical of Bowen, intensifies the atmosphere[10]. When the old couple decides to spend as little time in the house as possible, the weather outside seems to become more sinister: "We now seldom saw the sun; it was sultry weather. The trees became dark as though full of smoke." (BOS, 188)

The damaged furniture, the moved objects, the turned down clothes and papers – that is how they first notice Hobart's presence. Then, they start "seeing" him and hearing his laughter. Arthur and his wife (somehow her name is never mentioned in the text, which, in a way, makes her existence doubtful) cannot enjoy their home any more. Arthur starts preying on the ghost, like it seems to prey on them. Very soon one can see little difference between Arthur and Hobart, the life of Arthur being reduced to spectral existence. In the final episode, a collision between Arthur and the ghost is described, with a terrifying storm as the background. Imagining he is fighting with Hobart and following him outside, Arthur falls from the jetty "like a stone" and kills himself (BOS, 192).

From the very beginning, the deadly end Arthur will face is implied by his destination – the West Country, this is where he had always dreamt to live. But the West is considered to be a symbol of death, the portal to the netherworld, so, initially, Arthur's moving west was meant to become his last journey.

The first thing that strikes the eye about the setting and refers it to the Big House tradition is the isolation of the house and its seeming peacefulness: "And outdoors, nothing but the water, and across that nothing else but woods going steep up, as they did also behind our house. Few from the village came that way. No one to look in on us – so we thought!" (BOS, 184). The imminent danger lurks in the very first descriptions of the house, and the characters' being there "right away off by [them]selves" increases the sense of alertness.

Another feature of an Anglo-Irish Big House story which is evident in "The Claimant" is the characters' great attachment to the place and the strong sense of property they have: "Arthur almost cared for the place past reason" (BOS, 186), he thought that "a man should stay by his own home" (BOS, 188), and with that letter, he was hit "right in his sense of property" (BOS, 190). Hobart also seemed to be attached to the house. In his second letter he wrote: "It's my fate, my passion and my inheritance. MINE. And no one shall cheat me of it" (BOS, 185). The

---

10 Many critics have emphasised the close relation of weather depicted in Bowen's fiction and the emotions her characters have, for example, they use expressions such as "emotional heat" (Christensen, 91) or "emotional freeze" (Walshe, 135).

capitalized pronoun "MINE" and the word "passion" used in it suggest that the sender is closely connected with the place and moreover that this connection borders on mania.

Thirdly, in the short story, there is ambiguity in the matter of ownership, which is so important to the Anglo-Irish Big House discourse, and also the fear of dispossession. The claimant or the ghost of the dispossessed owner – P. St. J. Hobart (in addition, coming from Australia, another colonized land) – reflects what the English colonizers in Ireland would fear most of all – the Irish claiming their right to their land and to their country, which is what haunts their homes, their history and their literature.

Finally, the feeling of guilt and shame pervades the short story. The awareness of the unrightful occupancy of the land where their houses stand and of their power drawn "from a situation that shows an inherent wrong" made the Anglo-Irish feel the guilt even centuries after the Act of Union (BC, 453). Similarly, even if Arthur and his wife became the owners of the place by fair means, instead of possessing themselves of the house they become possessed by its history.

2. The Big House in *A World of Love*

The Irish Big House is the major setting and a major symbol in Bowen's novel *A World of Love*. The book was published in 1955 but the action takes place in the late thirties and focuses on the history of the house and its inhabitants. The country mansion Montefort is inhabited by the Danby family, Lilia, Fred and their two daughters, twenty-year-old Jane and twelve-year-old Maud. The house, however, belongs to Antonia, who sometimes comes to stay there. The short flashback at the beginning of the book briefs the reader on the complicated relationships connecting the characters. It turns out that Lilia was the fiancée of Antonia's cousin Guy, the previous owner of the house who was killed at World War I, and Fred is an illegitimate son of Antonia's uncle. After Guy's death, Antonia had been taking care of Lilia and later married her off to Fred, who, together with the wife, got the house to live in and the land to farm. To crown it all, Antonia turns out to have had romantic feelings towards Guy: she appears to have been in love with him, like Lilia. And like Lilia she was aware of another woman in Guy's life. The old love letters discovered by Jane in the attic unbury the family history of unconsummated loves and unsettle the seemingly peaceful atmosphere in the house.

Montefort is a decaying Anglo-Irish gentry estate, which immediately makes it fall within the convention of a Big House story. Typically, decay and ruin are inherent in the very notion of the Anglo-Irish Big House and usually stand for the decline of the class. Nevertheless, *A World of Love*, unlike *The Last September*, does not assume a socio-historical perspective and no tension between classes is represented: "the house exists most often with a certain disembodiment, as a form of the Anglo-Irish residence in decline, rather than as a place with any recognizable social, economic, or political resonances" (Kreilkamp 1998, 169). Still, the Big House remains an important figure of the novel and its symbolical significance is worth being revealed and discussed.

As was mentioned before, Bowen assigns to houses the importance of characters. She has a peculiar sense of place, devoting much of her literary talent to depicting unsympathetic environments. And although different from other houses discussed, the Big House remains the focal point of the novel's symbolic structure, weaving together its themes and motifs.

2.1 Uncanniness of the Houses: Insecurity and Troubling Uncertainty

The setting in *A World of Love* is opposed to that of *The Death of the Heart*, being set in the Irish countryside instead of London, in a country mansion instead of a city house and in the summer heat instead of the winter cold. Nevertheless, there predominates the same uncanny atmosphere, unsettling and tense, as in the novel previously discussed.

In *A World of Love*, there are two houses depicted: an old country mansion called Montefort and a renovated castle, both located in Ireland. Montefort represents the traditional Big House topos of a ruin in the landscape: with "an air of having gone down", "impoverished", with trees felled and façade carrying "a ghost of style" (WL, 9), the old mansion presents a blind end and looks deserted, so that people are surprised finding it is actually inhabited by the Danby family.

In her writing, Bowen often uses personification: the country is "accustomed", Ireland can feel "amazement" and the door "no longer knew hospitality" (WL, 9). But, in her Irish novels, as well as in the novels set in England or France, the house is the main object being personified as if to look like a living creature. First of all, in *A World of Love*, the house has a face. Moreover, it has a face that is "half-asleep" and "drowned" in the light (WL, 10). So, once the house has been considered alive, it is immediately recognized dead, drowned or put to sleep under the influence of a magical spell.

Another Irish novel, *The Last September*, also features a house with a face: "something unremembered about the face of the house, some intensification of the silence surrounding it, or perhaps simply Lois's figure standing there on the steps – made the place different" (LS, 25). An additional example of a house associated with a face can be found in *Bowen's Court*: "With buildings, as with faces, there are moments when the forceful mystery of the inner being appears" (BC, 20). From the very beginning, in its animation, the house, thus, is connected with a mystery.

The house in *A World of Love* is "dreadful" (WL, 12, 17), "terrible" (13), it is unnaturally silent and desolate: "the red doors, ajar, all seemed caught by a spell in the act of opening", "a visible silence filled the place", "the unprecedent loneliness of the afternoon looked out, as through eyelets cut in a mask, from the archways of the forsaken dovecote", even the sky was "uninhabited" (WL, 43). The inside of the house does not look much friendlier than the outside: the rooms are mantled with "tricky dusk" (WL, 13) and "clashing silence" (WL, 17), there is a creepy stillness around the house, and not a rustle anywhere. Strips of flypaper hang from the kitchen ceiling without swaying. The life in the house is framed in the doorways like a snapshot, and time seems to have stopped there. One can notice that there has been little change about the house, little innovation: there is an old dinted kitchen table, a roaring range in a blackened cave, no boilers or plumbing installed. "Rusty doors", "sealed-up Venetian window", "mossy road", "rutted track", "poor fence", "broken-walled garden" (WL, 9) – both the outside and inside of the house give away its decay.

However, there is something more about the house than just being old and going down, there is something about its atmosphere, which is "highly charged", in Neil Corcoran's words (2004, 65): "the air around them felt […] overintensified, strange" (18) and "wronged" – "either too empty or too full" (45). Familiar objects and individuals are endowed with strange characteristics, and the home is portrayed as a domain of secrecy and hostility. Importantly, the symbol of the house's decay and dereliction is the attic, where heaps of old things, broken and dusty, are buried and left to rot; where "everything was derelict, done for, done with" (WL, 27). It is where Jane feels being summoned to, sent for by somebody or something the house is full of. It is where she first feels oppressed by "the wreckage left by the past" (WL, 27).

The strikingly intense presence of the house makes it almost omnipresent. The acute sense of place is achieved by means of characters' consciousness of being inside or outside the building. The place is central, but what is even more important is the relation of people to the place, the unease between place and personality. Lilia dislikes the house, finds it terrible and dreadful; as for Antonia, "something monstrous seemed to her to be under her own roof" (WL, 18). Lilia has a neurosis about anyone standing outside the door and has had this sense since she came to live there: she feels "besieged, under observation or in some way even under threat" (WL, 52). Although the house's name implies protection and stability, it tends to unsettle the notion of stability itself, to settle the sense of insecurity within the four walls of the house.

Insecurity can be discerned at the level of the language ("In this heat how can I know what I am?", WL, 12 or "You're far too quick to assume that people are dead", WL, 37) – Bowen's style exhibits contrast, clearness and vagueness at the same time. She often uses apostrophes to blur the boundaries between the living and the dead. For example, when Lilia is in the garden, she addresses Guy as if he were alive and present, as if he could reply to her question. Also, Jane, while reading and rereading the letters, seems to talk to their author as well. And, finally, the night after the fête, Antonia addresses somebody but not Fred, who is helping her to get Jane to bed: "Our blood, his and mine, thought Antonia, roundabout by way of the byblow Fred. Asleep and besotted Jane, wine on her breath, made a point for the confluence of lost bright forces. Antonia cried out: 'She should have been his daughter!' The words were out – under them, Jane slept on unstirred. On the stove top there sizzled drip from a kettle. After some time: 'Were you speaking to me?' Fred asked. 'I – I am not sure,' faltered Antonia." (WL, 80).

On the whole, we may observe that Montefort is not only distinguished by its decline and dilapidation, by its isolation, but that it engenders the feeling of insecurity in its inhabitants. Being monstrously animated the house inspires inexplicable fear and anxiety.

On the other hand, the old and ruinous Montefort is opposed to the restored castle. The opposition between them is established from the first episode, which describes Lady Latterly's luxurious demesne. The castle which had been long empty and in disrepair before it was purchased by the nouveau riche aristocrat was turned into an "unusually banal Irish castle" (WL, 57). Now it is richly furnished and decorated, with "no trace of anything having been touched or used" (WL, 56). In fact, it reminds Jane of a theatre, as the rooms look unreal, and everything seems to be possible there: "Here she was, spirited out of Montefort into this foreign dimension of the castle, in which nothing, no one could be unreal enough" (WL, 57). The castle itself turned into a spectral space where reality became speculative.

The pointed unreality of the castle and the possibility of the most incredible occurrences taking place there lay a foundation for the later appearance of Guy's spectre noticed by Jane. Thus, the fact that the castle is not a ruin, like Montefort, does not make it less uncanny. On the contrary, the interior of the house itself looks spectral, liminal, caught between day and night, light and darkness:

> The bedroom gained still more unreality by now seeming trapped somewhere between day and night – this marvel of marbling and mirror-topping, mirror-building-in and

prismatic whatnots being at the moment a battleground of clashing dazzling reflections and refractions. Crystal the chandelier dripped into the sunset; tense little lit lamps under peach shades were easily floated in upon by the gold of evening. Day had not done with the world yet; trees were in the conspiracy. The outdoors, light-shot, uncannily deepening without darkening, leaned through the too-large windows – a blinding ray presently splintered over the dressing table. (WL, 56)

This long passage is quite interesting from the point of view of the language used. The repetition of the sound [m] in "marvel of marbling and mirror-topping, mirror-building-in…", [r] in "reflections and refractions", [l] in "little lit lamps" and others makes the text sound almost poetical and gives it a mysterious touch. Apart from alliteration, the choice of words in the rooms' description ("mirror", "prismatic", "seeming", "reflections", "blinding", etc.) is remarkable and may suggest the illusiveness of the space or rather a distortion of its perception by the characters.

Therefore, the castle, too, is uncanny and engenders a feeling of uncertainty. The uncanny here suggests a state of suspension between the world "as comforting or re-assuring and terrifying or absurd, because it involves a striving to regain a sense of coherence and harmony" (Connon, 12). And yet, Montefort is brought into the foreground of the novel and above all a great stress is put on its capability to produce the feeling of isolation, alienation and estrangement. Sunk in silence, with its hypnotic stillness, trance and stupor enveloping the inhabitants, the house seems to remain in a state of suspension or, to put it another way, it vividly evokes "the place and an atmosphere of people under spell" (Hartnett, 3).

To a great extent, *A World of Love* derives its setting and the atmosphere of isolation from *Bowen's Court*. In this outstanding work of hers, Bowen writes: "life in the big house, in its circle of trees, is saturated with character: this is, I suppose, the element of the spell. The indefinite ghosts of the past, of the dead who lived here" (Bowen "The Big House", 198). Like Bowen's Court, Montefort absorbed the peculiarly ambivalent cultural history of the Anglo-Irish. As a consequence of a series of social and political breakdowns, "the idea of society and the assumption of stability have never been securely lodged in Irish experience" (Deane, 12). Ambivalence is typical of the Anglo-Irish, as they are used to feeling as semi-strangers. And Bowen may owe the uncanny liminality of her characters and places they inhabit to her Anglo-Irish background.

The exploration of uncertainty within the novel is characteristic of Anglo-Irish literature. Andrew Carpenter claims that this sense of doubt and questioning, of uncertainty, this peculiar tension springs from the Anglo-Irish consciousness (173). It creates an effect of double perspective; the awareness of two cultures, two realities accounts for cultural as well as personal insecurity. Because of

Bowen's ascendancy and because she spent many years moving between Ireland and England, Bowen may be considered a part of Ireland but apart from the Irish. The richness of her novels' experience comes from seeing the world through inescapable double vision: "to write about life in Ireland is to reflect the ambiguities and tensions of life defined in double standards, double judgments and double visions" (Carpenter, 180). This uncertainty and anxiety generate unsettling tremors that can be felt reverberating throughout Bowen's fictive and autobiographical writing.

Particularly, the uncertainty permeates Bowen's novel *A World of Love,* which "epitomizes the inescapable ambivalence of her Anglo-Irish sensibility"(Kenney,79). No relationship is ever straightforward in her work. First of all, the uncertainty lies in the matter of ownership. Montefort belongs to Antonia, but the Danbys are neither tenants, nor caretakers. Their status is uncertain, "never secure, never defined" (WL, 13). Lilia feels "either galled or weighed upon by the ambiguity" (WL, 13) and as for Fred, he can hardly be called "a ruler over his own house" (WL, 110). The situation of ambiguity, of being half hosts, half not, creates the atmosphere of liminality, uncanny uncertainty about the place and self.

Antonia, Fred and Lilia never talked about the past or about the terms of the Danbys' living in the house:

> Fred farmed the land, and paid across to Antonia a half share of such profits as could be made; he and his family lived in the house for nothing, the best room in it being kept for Antonia to occupy when and how she chose. Of this arrangement it had not yet been decided whether it did or did not work, still less if it were equitable or, if not so, not so at whose expense. One could only say, it had lasted for twenty-one years, owing perhaps partly to all parties' reluctance to sitting down and having anything out, or to binding themselves to anything hard-and-fast, or to thinking out anything better. (WL, 13–14)

Without doubt, owing land confers a sense of belonging (Foster, 26). Therefore, ambiguity in the matter of ownership disrupts this sense and leaves one in the midst of confusion.

Another uncanny element in Bowen's work is the characters' uncertainty in the recognition of death, their inability or reluctance to believe and accept the deadness of the loved and let the past be sealed: "death, yes, why not? – but deadness, no" (WL, 45). The "central" character of the novel, Guy, is absent, dead, and other characters are in a state of suspension. Everyone in the house, except for the youngest Maud, is aware of Guy's presence in their lives. But even Maud has become subject to the family obsession: she is always accompanied by her uncanny familiar, "the non-dimensional Gay David" (WL, 142), whose name may as well be a misrepresentation of the name of the previous Montefort owner.

In Bowen's novel, the dead maintain a forceful presence in the consciousness of the living, their lives being constructed by the thoughts and memories of the dead. It presents an unsettling distinction between life and death, their constant interweaving: "Bowen's writing is pervaded by the forces of dissolution and mourning. In fascinating and highly singular ways, her novels examine the disquieting truth that in the midst of life we are in death" (Bennett, Royle, xviii). Thus, the living are affected by the dead, or rather by their feelings to the dead, to the relationships with people who died. Bowen's characters cease to live their own lives but surrender to the past and sometimes to other peoples' memories, which they cannot any longer discern from theirs.

2.2 The Phantoms of the Big House

A World of Love is said to be "as close to being a ghost story as her novels were ever allowed to come" (Lee, 184). Bowen's characters are constantly surrounded by reminders of death and dying; the images of death and decay crystallize around the house which conveys a sense of menace and claustrophobia. In *A World of Love*, there are many allusions to death: the darkness, silence and emptiness which reign throughout the house and contribute to the aura of a tomb; the cataleptic stillness; the trance and stupor that envelopes the inhabitants; the heat leading to fast decay, the flies; the sight of sleeping Antonia, who resembles a dead body: her immobility, "unfresh surrounding air", "her face sealed by the resolution never […] to wake at all" (WL, 11); the muslin dress belonging to somebody dead displayed at the window at night, looking like a body of a hanged person.

But the element which most explicitly hints at death, or rather immortality, is the presence of Guy felt by the female inhabitants of Montefort. There are several times when his presence is registered: Guy appears to Antonia at the doorstep of the house, to Lilia in the garden and to Jane in Lady Latterly's castle. In all the cases, the appearance of the ghost contributes to spatial disjunction, but the first two cases are also marked by time disruption.

Antonia, as well as Lilia, feels the presence of the supernatural when she is overwhelmed by the memories of Guy and them being together. Everything around her seems to remind her of their past:

> Drawn she was, all but knowing why. Going to stand in the doorway, she was met at once by a windlike rushing towards her out of the dark – her youth and Guy's from every direction: the obelisk, avenue, wide country, steep woods, river below. […] A call or calling, now nearby, now from behind the skyline, was unlocatable as a corncrake's in uncut

grass. A rising this was, on the part of two who like hundreds seemed to be teeming over the land, carrying all before them. (WL, 77)

This passage illustrates how emotion is fixed through space and objects in it and how it shows a characteristically intense relation between person and place in the novel. The vision Antonia has originates in her inability to accept Guy's death, so, here, to "see" means to unconsciously remember. Things that make up the place cease to be just objects in the world and become an extension of Antonia's personal identity. When she crosses the borderline entering the house, not only does she transgress a spatial border, but she enters a different time scale. The doorstep she is standing on is symbolical and represents the border between the present and the past, the living and the dead.

The doorway as a heterotopian portal also appears in the passage where Lilia sees the ghost: "a door creaked; somebody had come in and was in this garden. But not again a sound, not a step – there ensued more than a silence of moss, sloth, airlessness and the exhausted river: something more than human was at intensity. In depth, dead-still, branches screened the doorway – of whom was this the ghost in the afternoon?" (WL, 97). The doorway, the path dividing the garden, the garden itself and many other places depicted in the novel also acquire features of liminality: "For as land knows, everywhere is a frontier; and the outposted few (and few are the living) never must be off guard." (WL, 79)

The presence of a ghost in fiction often points to family secrets or troubled sexuality. Barbara Creed claims that "the ghost points to secrets within the family or group; its presence reveals issues relating to troubled forms of sexual desire and to secret crimes" (Creed, xvi). When the spectre is male, continues Creed, it almost always assumes characteristics of the primal uncanny. The haunted house, the family home, is horrifying because it contains cruel secrets and has witnessed terrible deeds committed by family members against each other. The house, thus, becomes a symbolic space which gives rise to a sense of disquiet, unease and fear. A seemingly safe domestic space, appearing fortress-like in its physical solidity, but disturbed by secrets and fears, it is destabilized by the risk of their disclosure.

The haunting is even more persistent, claims Palmer, when the family secret is known to most or all family members and yet they do not talk about it (Palmer, 118). Things are often left unsaid in Montefort, they hang in the air, making the silence intense and the conversations elliptical and allusive. The family secrets raise the spectre of taboo and transgression with consequences for the identity of the characters: "Obstinate rememberers of the dead seem to queer themselves or show some sign of a malady; in part they come to share the dead's isolation, which it is not in their power to break down" (Palmer, 44).

In these two passages, the spectre seems to be a psychological phenomenon brought into being by the women's memories. The ghost of Guy is a psychological projection rather than a supernatural entity (O'Connor, 31–32). It emerges from within the everyday, the home and the self, rather than from the external world. All in all, the ghosts that Lilia and Antonia see are phantoms of their past life.

The episode when Jane feels the presence of Guy bears little resemblance to the previous apparitions. First of all, the vision of Guy cannot be evoked by Jane's memories of him, as he had died long before she was born. However, it may be conjured up by assimilating others' memories, taking them for her own ones: "That he had been with them, with her, was an unfettered fact – where is there perfection but in the memory?" (WL, 70). It is clear enough that Jane has little interest in the present moment but feels attraction for other people's past. She is interested in the dead more than in the living people around her: as she says, "one forgets people when they are always there" (WL, 94). It creates an atmosphere of atrophy and passivity, an oppressive sense of paralysis and a sense of being acted upon.

> She experienced the absolute calmness, the sense of there being almost no threat at all, with which one could imagine fighting one's way down a burning staircase – there was a licking danger, but not to her; cool she moved down between flame walls. Only, all went to heighten her striking power – and had she not struck when she spoke the name! It had left her lips and was in the room. Guy was among them. The recoil of the others – she did not for an instant doubt it was a recoil – marked his triumphant displacement of the air. She saw the reflection of crisis in each face, heard it in loudening, dropping then stopping voices. (WL, 65)

Jane herself becomes like a ghost, wearing an old dress from the trunk, absorbed by the world of the letters. Kathie, the servant, is not even sure if it was Jane she saw in the yard or if it was a vision. Antonia also notes that Jane is in a kind of a trance. According to Terry Castle, "the 'ghost' of the dead or absent person, conceived as a kind of visionary image or presence in the mind, takes on a new and compelling subjective reality" (136). In this reality "absence is preferable to presence. […] The dead are more interesting than the living. […] Objects are more compelling than people. (Objects evoke memories; people disturb them.)" (Castle, 136).

Over a few days Jane has been engaged with imagining the past, but not actually living in the present. She chooses to stay in the world of love she created with the help of those letters. At the dinner in Lady Latterly's castle, Jane's main preoccupation is learning about Montefort of the old days, about Guy, rather than talking about the present or future life of the country. Other people at the party have little significance to her, they may gain importance only as mediators between Guy and her: "while these men helped to compose Guy, they remained tributary to him and less real to Jane – that is, as embodiments – than was he" (WL, 68). On the whole, the presence of Guy is more desired by Jane than the presence of any living people and the past is more important than the present. Jacqueline Genet rightly points out that here the "implicitly claimed richness of the past is in sharp contrast with the explicitly stated emptiness of the present" (Genet, 164).

For Bowen, ghosts serve as an important point of conjunction between her modernism and the Big House tradition. In the analysis of Big House stories, Rauchbauer uses the term "tale-type" (182). He claims that with the social decline of the Big House, many characters have a tendency of myth-making. Rauchbauer sees one of the reasons of myth-making or gross misrepresenting of the reality in a compensation for a drab existence. One of the decaying house themes is the meditation of a member of the Big House expressing his or her existential frustration (Rauchbauer, 187). Trapped in the routine, Bowen's characters feel claustrophobic inside their houses, their memory and their lives.

Also, through preoccupation with internal and external ghosts, Bowen's modernism is centrally tied to her reinvention of Gothic conventions (Wurtz, 120). In the passage where Jane sees the ghost of Guy, Bowen uses parodic reference to the Gothic style. Firstly, Lady Latterly's house is a parody of the Gothic castle haunted by unquiet spirits: instead of haunting an old gloomy medieval castle, the ghost appeared in a tasteless, ostentatiously decorated manor. Secondly, as Lee Kovacs claims, the haunter and haunted can only connect through death or in the face of death (3). Only in this case it was the death of a moth scorched with the candle light and pinched to death by the Irish butler.

All in all, it cannot be denied that Bowen's writing is concerned with death and dissipation, her novels presenting dissolutions at the level of personal identity, patriarchy, social conventions and language (Bennett, Royle, xix). The family house, in Bowen's fiction, is no image of confidence and continuity but, as Paul Gilbert puts it, it is "a site of dissolution and dispersion" (Gilbert, 207–208). The house, in Bowen, becomes a ghost itself, and the life in it is reduced to spectral existence.

2.3 Space and Time Relations in the Novel

What produces this uncanny effect? In *A World of Love* Bowen puts the question as follows: "Was it the place itself, her mistrust of Ireland or the uncanny attentiveness of the country which kept her [Lilia's] nerves ever upon the stretch?" (WL, 53). Comparing *A World of Love* to *The House in Paris* or *The Death of the Heart* it is evident that it is not a matter of Ireland, nor of the location in the countryside. In *The House in Paris* the action takes place mainly in the cities of France and England but the same atmosphere of uncanniness can be observed in the houses. Thus, it is not in a particular house, not just Montefort, not the house in Paris, rue Sylvestre Bonnard, but, generally, in Bowen's concept of the house or home space disrupted by the recurrence from the past of their inhabitants.

The houses are haunted and the people who own or inhabit them are possessed by the images of their past. Lilia's lover died, killed in the war. But in addition to the grief of the loss, since their farewell at the station she has lived with the vague knowledge or strong suspicion of his cheating on her. The secret of Guy's unfaithfulness haunts the domestic space of the house and deepens the trauma of its inhabitants. Even after many years the women remain in the power of their memories. They are haunted because of "the past not being yet over" (HP, 50) or because of the "not-to-be-settled old scores" (WL, 35).

Talking about time and space relationships in *A World of Love*, Vera Kreilkamp claims that the novel critiques the obsession with the past (Kreilkamp 1998, 173). On the other hand, the gloomy orientation to the past in Bowen's novel may be explained by her belonging to the Ascendancy. The Anglo-Irish tradition often treats the relationship between the past and the present with the shaping role of the past. It features the continuing process of its revision, and one of the prevailing themes is fulfilment of a particular place with a specific history, placing the action in the perspective of an older world (Gilbert, 207). The Big House culture represents the past's hold on the present, the struggle of one against the other. "I know of no house (no house that has not changed hands) in which, while the present seems to be there forever, the past is not pervadingly felt" (BC, 29). Each of these houses has "the startling, meaning and abstract clearness of a house [...] in which something important occurred once, and seems, from all evidence, to be occurring still" (BC, 30).

The Big House is a haunted place by definition; it exists "as a receptacle of illusion, as a richly evocative symbol of its occupants' encapsulation in the past" (Kreilkamp 1998, 168). It is the site where "issues concentrate", "an uneasy repository of the past, neither crypt nor monument, where what has died can never really pass and what lives cannot escape the grasp of the dead" (Wurtz, 120).

At first sight, one may have an impression of "almost total irrelevance of Time" (WL, 21) in the novel. The action seems to take place in a timeless world: there are no dates mentioned, only days of the week and hours, the calendar hanging on the kitchen wall is of the year before, the only clock often stops, and nobody seems to know or care what time it is. The only person in the house who cares about knowing the correct time is twelve-year-old Maud, who worships her toy Big Ben and tunes it in to strike. The rest will guess or feel by instinct what time or day it is. Even the old letters that Jane finds in the attic are headed only by day names; there are no envelopes or stamps, so it is impossible to say when they were actually posted. Nevertheless, the impression of time's insignificance is deceptive. The "datelessness" of the letters may imply that, in the house, "time was being kept in some other way" (WL, 34). And this way is precisely what is crucial for understanding the reasons for the space uncanniness.

In Bowen, time is central; it is often capitalized and, like house, it is treated as a separate character. The defective clock may be perceived as a symbol of defective, distorted time with its leaps into the past, slowing pace or freezing still. Its striking is used to signal the change in the time-frame or focalisation, and the portrait of Guy hanging near the clock suggests he is connected with the time distortion. The circular structure observed in *A World of Love,* where the action takes place during a few days in the present with recurrent flashbacks to the past, emphasizes the power that time has over the characters and shows how easily the boundary between the present and past can be crossed in the novel.[11]

Marcella O'Connor points out that time is central in Elizabeth Bowen's Irish fiction because "her novels and stories constitute a metafictional account of the dispossessed Anglo-Irish identity in the twentieth century" (5). She warped the experience of time in her fiction in order to disrupt ontological stability in the narrative and to show how the relations of character to setting and of character to others are mediated by the force of time. "In this novel Elizabeth Bowen has stressed the Big House's power to multiply itself in the imagination and memory, so as to take on a new significance there, and put off the moment of epiphany, of recognition and acceptance of reality" (Genet, 174).

According to Ann Owens Weekes, Bowen's Irish writing features a representation of dislocation and dispossession as a natural condition of life (1990, 83). Even so, it should be noted that the dislocation occurs both in space and time and dispossession does not only and so much mean deprivation of ownership as rather a kind of exorcism, the process of getting rid of the burdensome past. The Gothic element represents a response to the characters' psychological disturbances. Traces of unresolved past events or the ghosts of those who died too suddenly to be properly mourned "possess those who are seeking to get on with the task of living" (Whitehead, 6). The ghost is associated with the disruptive return

---

11 Only young Maud, with her devotion to the clock, is the one in the house not overcome by the past and thus not afraid of its power.

of buried secrets or repressed truths, that is why the literary ghost may be called the "truth-event" awaiting ontological determination (Thurston, 6).

2.4 The Inhabitants and Their Trauma

Assuming that the representation of the house is the correlative of the inhabitants' psychological condition, it is clear that the threat felt is not objective reality but a manifestation of the characters' disturbed mental state caused by their memories of the past. They are vulnerable to the ambience and forced to confront the surrounding world, which seems different from what it actually is, but, in the effect, the perception of otherness is directed inwards.

In *A World of Love*, the portrayal of the everyday conveys a sense of anxiety defamiliarizing the familiar, for instance, the light is "unfamiliar" (WL, 9) or the summer is "unknown" (WL, 9). Jane's going to the places mentioned in the letters, the obelisk, the river bank, etc., and reading about them seem to be part of a ritual summoning the spirits. The familiar places gain a new meaning, new importance in the view of the history disclosed in the letters: "The particular secret of the place where Jane lay was that it was pre-inhabited. An ardent hour of summer had gone by here – yes, here, literally where she was, to her certain knowledge. Evidence was in the breast of her dress, the letter." (WL, 48)

Also, the summer heat looks and feels like winter cold: the heat stands over the land "like a white-hot sword, causing an apprehensive hush" (WL, 20), an eerie "snowlike reflection" (WL, 20) comes from the white buildings and, with its stone floor, the kitchen looks cool without being so.

The night after Jane mentioned her finding "everything was magnified and distorted; everything had its way with the unpent senses; the lamp [...] gave warning by an earsplitting crack, and the flame itself [...] crimsonly stuttered inside the gloom it made like an evil tongue" (WL, 76). The senses had sharpened, and everyone felt under pressure, felt intensity in the air: "tonight was a night which had changed hands, going back again to its lordly owners: time again was into the clutch of herself and Guy. Stamped was the hour, as were their others." (WL, 77)

The author draws upon the language and motifs of alterity. She destabilizes the concept of home in order to represent the other and the self, exposing the anxieties. Uncanniness becomes synonymous with alterity, the ghost that haunts subjectivity. Unaware of the loss, Jane interposed herself between the older women and their personal memories, turning the house into a space filled with strangers rather than family, on constant alert against the invasion of the past: "What

115

she thought, no one had thought of asking until this morning – but then, what an alien she'd seemed to be!" (WL, 45).

The characters are caught in this world of ruin and decay, fated by isolation and denial of love, spellbound. What seems to be a definition of landscape turns out to be a "highly sophisticated definition of self" (Carpenter, 176). The uncanny suggests an unsettling of the feeling of comfort and reassurance in one's home, but also in oneself. Architecture takes the place of psychology (Kreilkamp 2009, 15). The perturbed relationship between the characters and their familiar world, the troubled sense of home and self-certainty is a result of a traumatic experience of loss.

Bowen's style is more insistent on registering loss than the style of any other Big House writers. However, in *A World of Love*, losses are not framed within a national historical trauma as it was in her early works: the decay in Montefort frames and foregrounds more central "psychic losses" (Kreilkamp 1998, 171). Bowen's novels are "stories of the need to be" (Kenney 1975, 18), describing the acquisition of knowledge through loss and the entrance into selfhood. Moreover, in her novels, Bowen is rather concerned with the self's response to the experience of loss, than with the loss itself.

The destruction or decay of the house is the ultimate symbol of loss. The world is a troubling place, and the subject is searching for home, rootedness, meaning to cling to. After several unsuccessful attempts to get a job and earn her living Lilia was married off to Fred. Weak, dull-witted and subordinate – that is how her family see her. After Guy's death she could only have a home after marrying a man she hardly knew. She was merely a complement to the house which she has disliked since that time.

In his essay on Elizabeth Bowen's fiction, Derek Hand underlines the peculiar conception of home the Anglo-Irish have; he stresses how important the idea of having a home is for them: "The Anglo-Irish cannot live without a palpable connection to home: like flowers they die when they are uprooted from the soil" (Hand, 69). To have a home, be the owner of a Big House has a huge meaning in Anglo-Irish culture. And even when Big Houses lost their glory, they were maintained by struggle and sacrifice: "Sons were recalled from college, or never went there; daughters, undowered, stayed unwed; love-marriages had to be interdicted because money was needed to prop the roof." (Bowen "The Big House", 197). Hermione Lee calls it "the Ascendancy's fanatical commitment to property" (ix).

When Antonia tried to persuade Lilia that she should marry Fred, what was most convincing was the promise to have a home. Similarly, Fred agreed to marry a woman he hardly knew because the marriage would make him the master of a Big House. However, their expectations have not been fully fulfilled and now they are tied to the house and cannot easily escape.

The revival of the past in *A World of Love* to a great extent is caused by the discovery of the letters, thus unburying the family history of unconsummated loves and unfulfilled expectations. The letters were found by Jane (or possibly found Jane) in the attic of the mansion. The symbolism of the attic echoes into deep layers of the unconscious. It is generally known that an attic serves for storing old things which belong to the past but which one cannot easily get rid of. The role it plays within a house emphasizes its connection with an individual mind and its ability to retain. The attic stands for memory, storing one's ideas and thoughts which have been sent away, hidden, but which one still clings to. Finding something in an attic means discovering memories from the past. Those memories are embodied in the letters. The focus on the attic can indicate that it is time for the protagonists to sort out their lives, to bring to light the secrets of the past, to exorcise its spirits.

The love letters are the narrative core of the novel. They manage to stir and bring to the surface what has long reached its point. The characters' lives become determined by forms of trans-generational haunting; for years, traumatic memories have existed in a kind of frozen state, untouched by the passage of time. And now, when they are once again exposed to a painful situation, the discovery of the letters, uncanny feelings are evoked. Alan J. Parkin, relying on G. H. Bower's state-dependent theory, claims that the emotional content of memories can decide how accessible they are (Parkin, 46–47). Parkin states that the mood experienced at the time of an event becomes part of the memory of that event. Thus, the retrieval of the event is more lively if the person's current mood is similar to that associated with the events. Like the return to the old house for Mrs. Drover in *The Demon Lover,* where the key element is also a letter from a dead lover, the return to the old family history for Antonia and Lilia is "a threshold experience" activating the "dormant hysteria" (Hughes, 412), the recovery from which would require them to revisit the past.

Only the discovery of the letters and talking the matter over for the first time make Lilia realise her loss: "Loss had been utter: not till today had she wholly taken account. Guy was dead, and only today at dinner had she sorrowed him." (WL, 50). The loss of Guy was so difficult for Lilia that her mind sealed away this traumatic episode. The event was unconsciously retained in the mind but it still affected conscious thought. It lurked beneath the consciousness and caused neurotic states, anxiety and fear. Her conscious awareness was blocked in order not to experience the painful effects of her loss. Thus, her memories have been repressed until the discovery of the letters, when finally she allowed her feelings to be expressed: "accumulated, the panic of twenty years broke in a wave over Lilia" (WL, 89).

While Lilia's memories are repressed, Antonia tries to suppress hers. Martha McGowan claims that Antonia helped Lilia out of sense or responsibility for her (58), but, at long last, it is rather guilt than the desire to help the weak or unjustly treated. Antonia deliberately pushes her memories of those days out of awareness to avoid responsibility for taking away Lilia's fiancé. According to M. M. Tatar, a ghost may be at once the spectre of conscience and of consciousness: "The ghosts brought to life by the voice of the conscience are, in the literal sense of the term, familiar spirits" (167).

Lilia too can be feeling guilt towards Guy after marrying Fred. Her neurosis related to the house, the feeling of being under observation might be her blaming herself of unfaithfulness to Guy, of living in his house with another man, living the life Guy was devoid of. The "monomania" in the house Lilia mentions can be a signal of bad conscience with its fearful summonses and a wish to change her life. Lilia starts the changes with the new hair cut. On the other hand, Lilia's dash to have her hair cut may as well be explained by her unconscious wish to forget. According to primitive beliefs, the hair absorbs knowledge and has memory. On cutting her hair Lilia tries to get rid of unnecessary memories that make her suffer.

Another person who suffers from the unforgotten past, for whom the letters are "thorn in the flesh" is Fred, Lilia's husband (WL, 111). He is overtaken by jealousy, as everyone in the house seems to be obsessed with Guy: Antonia, his wife and now even his daughter. The estrangement is growing between him and his family, and he feels himself an odd one out, an unfortunate double of the former Montefort owner whose place he would never be able to take. Fred realises that the relationship he and Lilia have is not their own, he is just Guy's substitute and is not regarded as himself but as the other. This, too, incites a conflict within himself.

Antonia, demonstrating her imperious manipulative manner, wants to hold everything under her control – the management of Montefort, Fred and Lilia's family matters. She arranged their marriage for her own benefit, but their falling in love with each other has never been her plan. She does not let Fred forget about their agreement and treats Lilia merely as a thing, a part of her possessions. But perhaps the most painful thing for Fred is to share Jane (for whom he feels almost an incestous desire) with Antonia. Antonia spends much time with the girl and has great influence on her. It is Antonia who paid for Jane's education, and Lilia notices that she even starts talking like Antonia. Here, the feeling of uncertainty also reigns in the matter of parenthood and family identity.

Uncertainty and insecurity make one's identity ambivalent and fluid: "the modern ghost story often gravitated around the self as dubious centre" (Thurston, 96). But, at the same time, the uncertainty about the world and self encourages the individual's search for meaning and order. Lilia had been playing the role of Guy's beloved for more than twenty years all the time suspecting that there was another woman but persuading herself not to think about it. The appearance of Guy has been looked forward to only in the hope of getting the answer, of knowing who was that person at the station Guy had been waiting for.

> It was not to be thought of, so never was. Had it been seen again, that awaited face? Had she come to the train, that last-moment comer? If so, who was she; if not, what was she not? Was she – did she exist? Did he expect her, did he invent her? There had stood he and Antonia, jibing at one another up to the end. 'You never know, you know.' Better uncertainty; best no answer. Who desires to know what they need not? So why continue to wonder, so why suffer? Yes, but if not the Beloved, what was Lilia? Nothing. Nothing was left to be. (WL, 96)

Although Lilia assumes it is better not to know, not to wonder, the question keeps coming back. Having been suppressed, the wish to know or the knowledge itself is transferred into fears, worries and anxieties that make Lilia suffer for so many years.

Clearly, Lilia and Antonia are possessed by the past, and the uncanniness they feel is the result of their painful memories (loss and guilt). But Jane is different. The presence of Guy that she feels is the embodiment of her "predisposition toward love", in O'Connor's words (31). It is not accidental that Jane goes to the obelisk wearing that anachronistic dress and hairdo to read the letters. The Obelisk is the symbol of family history on the one hand, but, on the other hand, it has a pronounced phallic insistence. According to Jacques Lacan, the phallus is a residue of desire, a demand for love (Mitchel, Rose, 80–84). It is the signifier of the desire of the Other: "it is in order to be the phallus, that is to say, the signifier of the desire of the Other, that the woman will reject an essential part of her femininity [...] through masquerade. It is for what she *is not* that she expects to be desired as well as loved" (italics mine – O.L) (Mitchel, Rose, 84). Jane's masquerade, putting on the old dress probably worn by the woman who Guy was in love with, is her unconscious desire to be what she is not, to be the woman, to be loved and desired. In her developing sexuality, she seeks a world of love and romance, undergoes a kind of sexual initiation – a recurring motif in Bowen's fiction.

Lacan links anxiety to Freud's concept of the uncanny. According to Lacan, anxiety is a "way of sustaining desire when the object is missing" (430). Anxiety arises when the subject is confronted by the desire of the Other and does not know what object he or she is for that desire. Lacan also links anxiety to the concept of lack; the anxiety arises when this lack is itself lacking. Falling in love with Guy's letters, Jane tries to meet this lack and to fill her want of romance.

The heat also may be understood not only in physical terms but as the heat of desire, love and passion (Bennett, 107). This is most true in the case of Jane, whose desires are ignited by the letters. Even the title, *A World of Love*, and the epigraph seem to confirm that, in part, the anxiety permeating the novel is a result of unexpressed or hidden desire: "There is in us a world of Love to somewhat, though we know not what in the world that should be ... Do you not feel yourself drawn by the expectation and desire of some Great Thing?" (WL, 8). In addition, throughout the novel, one can notice the use of phrases expressing wish, like the only citation from the letters given in the novel: "If only YOU had been here" (WL, 48), or the sentences starting with "I wish" (WL, 73, 99, 125, 137).

But the heat is bound to terminate in thunderstorm, both literally and figuratively. Jane's mounting the attic in search of adventures anticipates the crisis: "Something has got to happen" (WL, 24). According to Lotman, an upward movement is a movement for transformation (218–220); the distance height is associated with means distance in time – the events of more than twenty years old. Unlike older women who are encapsulated in the past, Jane is a mobile character who can move from one environment to another across the temporal boundary. Like Mary in "The Happy Autumn Fields" she can cross "the impenetrable border between two different realities: the real world and the world of the past" (Kędra-Kardela, 178).

On opening the old trunk, a sort of Pandora's box, Jane lets out what, at first sight, is better to be left alone but what eventually liberates the family from its burden of the past. Just as Fred wants Antonia to clear the attic to make more space available, memories over-cramming the lives of the people need to be cleared up to make room for the future: "Life works to dispossess the dead, to dislodge and oust them. Their places fill themselves up; later people come in; all the room is wanted" (WL, 44). The wish to make more space in the attic and in life testifies to the characters' longing for renewal.

The letters for the first time motivate Lilia and Fred to have an open talk about the past. While avoiding certain important questions, they have become even more insistent. The crisis provoked by Jane's discovery was necessary for all of them to move on with their lives: "Survival seemed more possible now, for having spoken to one another had been an act of love" (WL, 105).

A World of Love is the only novel by Bowen where eventually the spirits have been exorcised. The spell is broken with nine chimes of the clock: "But now came Now – the imperative, the dividing moment, the spell-breaker – all else was thrown behind, disappeared from reality, was over. Time swooped as it struck" (WL, 129). The removal of the spell changes the space of the house, which seems to be restoring its order: "The room righted its balance, causing objects to seem to be slipping back into what had been their position" (WL, 130). The painful past has been worked through, revived, re-lived and then buried for good. Jane has liberated the family through "exorcising" Guy's spirit: "He came back, through Jane, to be let go. It was high time." (WL, 135).

The spell removal is marked by the weather change: coolness comes instead of the heat, the sky looks like one big cloud and is ready to burst with rain. After the days of heat, the thunderstorm metaphorically acts as a reflection of the intense atmosphere in the house that needed a crisis. With the letters burnt, Antonia's power over the Montefort inhabitants seems to have disappeared, too. Her significance for them is not as it used to be: she loses her power even over Jane, who will soon meet her love, a real man called Richard. The magic of the muslin dress fades away, leaving only "the smell of banishment" and "pastness" (WL, 134), and the four-leaved clover found by Harris near the obelisk bodes well for the future.

The unconscious representations of the trauma are encoded and stored in memories, and these unconscious memories appear in the form of intrusive images and hallucinatory visions. The visions that Lilia and Antonia had were provoked by the trauma of loss – "the figuration of the immemorial – of what can be neither remembered nor forgotten" (Bennett, 112). This "immemorialism" is the very space of the novel.

The Big House takes the form of a text, read and interpreted by different characters (Genet, 170). Their interpretation depends on their experience, their past, especially the past that makes them feel uncomfortable, reduplicating it in the experience of the house itself. And while Jane reads the Big House as a text of Love, the rest of the characters find it far less pleasing. For Antonia, it is a text of power, manipulation, but also of guilt. And Lilia reads it as a text of loss and unfulfilled expectations. Ignoring the pain instead of facing it, repressing feelings and desires, inevitably leaves its stamp on her mental state affecting her sense of space. In this case, the house becomes a monument of trauma.

To conclude, *A World of Love* is "a novel troubled by subjectivism" (Austin, 80). The concept of home as a natural, organic place of comfort is challenged and its stability is upset. A multitude of representations are superimposed within it, and the Big House, in its ability to multiply itself, serves as a way to reflect these representations of the characters' individual consciousness.

Conclusion

The study sets out to examine the image of the house in Bowen's prose and to explore the uncanniness of domestic space in relation to the characters' identity. An attempt has been made to elucidate, through the use of psychoanalytical theory, how the house in Bowen's fiction becomes a representation of the characters' self and embodies their wishes, fears and losses. The study offers analysis of three of Bowen's novels (*The House in Paris*, *The Death of the Heart* and *A World of Love*) and twelve short stories, including those which have not been published until recently.

By addressing Bowen's work in terms of its relation to the uncanny, this study has sought to fill the gap in the existing criticism on Bowen, much of which is inconclusive. The book has sought to extend the discussion of the symbolic role of the house in Bowen's fiction and it has also sought to examine how traumatic experiences of the past are connected with the characters' perception of domestic space and how the crisis of their selves can be projected onto the house.

In this last chapter, it is necessary to review some of the main findings of the study. It has been found that Bowen's fiction, her novels as well as short stories, are centred on the house as the representation of human psyche and may be seen to constitute the focal point of her fiction. The readings of Bowen's oeuvre in this book have revealed that the uncanniness of domestic space is the result of the characters' misplacement of repressed wishes and fears from their internal world to the external environment and that the uncanny house in Bowen stands for her characters' traumatic experience of loss.

The research material gathered has suggested the focus of each chapter. Firstly, the concept of the uncanny and the causes of its emergence were explored. The analysis of theoretical sources allowed concluding that the uncanny is the experience of frightening uncertainty, disorientation and alienation of the subject. It includes the key notions of home, foreignness, everydayness, revelation and encounter with the other, boundary and liminality.

It was shown that the uncanny is psychologically conditioned and represents repressed anxieties and traumas, which manifest themselves through strange and terrifying images. The repetition or the return of these past images is mandatory within the uncanny and signals mental fixation on the trauma. This fixation produces identity crisis and causes disintegration of time and space perceived by the subject. Time becomes fragmentary and kaleidoscopic, non-linear and circular, whereas space acquires features producing fear and strange uncertainty, making the subject insecure in his or her own abode. However, the source of the strangeness and fear appears to be within the self and does not come from the outer world.

At the next stage, a study of practical material was carried out. The analysis of Bowen's novel *The House is Paris* and her short stories "The Needlecase", "Story Scene", "Making Arrangements" and "The Return" revealed that the house in Bowen is presented as a heterotopian portal; it provides an insight into other spaces and times through characters' memories and wishes. It also proved that time in Bowen is represented as duration: it is circular, with no beginning and no end, and it is measured by moments, which contain the past, the present and the future.

Also, the house appears to be a place of the intersection of the real and the imaginary; it is uncommon, unnatural, strangely animated and even antagonistic to its inhabitants. Its exceeding darkness, quietness and cold contribute to the atmosphere of uncanniness and the image of a trap pursues the characters once they enter the house. This state of things is due to the repressed anxieties and losses each of them undergoes. For Bowen's female characters, the house is made oppressive as a result of domesticization they try to resist in marriage. The death of a close person, adultery and orphanhood are among other traumatic experiences that disintegrate the characters' selves affecting their perception of domestic space.

Furthermore, the study of Bowen's novel *The Death of the Heart* and her short stories "The Apple Tree", "Home for Christmas", "The Cassowary" and "The Shadowy Third" helped to examine the role memory plays in the disintegration of domestic space in Bowen's fiction. It revealed that most of Bowen's characters suffer from reminiscences, they are haunted by memories that become a heavy burden and an awful curse in their lives. Once they are traumatized, Bowen's characters keep returning to the painful event in their memory or imagination and often feel the presence of the Other within themselves.

The difficulty that arises while investigating the causes of uncanniness lies in the fact that what is unconscious appears in a disguised form and what is repressed is expressed indirectly, in a displaced manner. Memories are usually distorted and demand special approach in the analysis, that is why a study of the characters' dreams and fantasies was undertaken. Dreams and fantasies replicate the initial trauma and allow the reader to disclose what is hidden. The interpretation of dreams helped to show how the domestic space of the novel becomes a repository of memory, a reflection of its inhabitants' personal identity disintegrated by death, homelessness or exile.

Finally, the analysis of Bowen's Big House fiction, the novel *A World of Love* and the short stories "Her Table Spread", "Sunday Afternoon", "Christmas Games" and "The Claimant" allowed us to explore the uncanniness of domestic space within the Anglo-Irish Big House tradition. The Gothic element inscribed in it represents a response to the characters' psychological disturbances, which are often connected with the ambiguity in terms of ownership and belonging to a place. The psychological projections such as ghosts stand for the unresolved past, the disruptive return of buried secrets or the repressed truths that await ontological determination.

Moreover, the study revealed that the Big House fiction literary pattern, which normally relies on social and historical conflict, in Bowen, appears to be different, rather focused on the inner psychological conflict of the characters. In the above-mentioned texts, the insecurity and lifelessness of domestic space signals at the inner instability and disintegration of the subject while the Big House becomes a symbol of loss, a monument to personal trauma.

Ultimately, then the main concern of this study was to show that the house in Bowen's fiction is not a place of confidence and continuity but a site of uncertainty and dissolution. The uncanniness of Bowen's houses comes from the traumatic experience of the characters, particularly from the experiences of orphanhood, homelessness and the death of a dear person. The traumatic experience of the loss causes uncertainty about the characters' identity and a crisis of their selves, which, in turn, appears to be the reason for space and time disintegration.

The findings of the study have opened a space for considering the role the uncanny plays in the works written not only by Bowen but also by other English and Anglo-Irish modernist writers. The concept of the uncanny, derived from Freud and developed by twentieth-century philosophers and critics, provides a more insightful reading of modernist fiction and gives a clearer comprehension of its various themes and ideas than other approaches. The uncanny proves to be a key to understanding modernism as the latter is centred on interiority, oriented at subjectivisation of time and space and externalization of consciousness. The modernist aesthetics of simultaneity, which attempts to retrieve the lost identity through the work of memory, combined with the recurring representation of alienation of the subject, makes the uncanny a master category of modernism.

Bibliography

1. Abrams, M. H. *A Glossary of Literary Terms*. Boston: Heinle & Heinle, 1999.
2. Adams, Timothy Dow. "'Bend Sinister': Duration in Elizabeth Bowen's *The House in Paris*". *The International Fiction Review* 7.1 (1980): 49–52.
3. Antze, Paul and Lambek, Michael, eds. *Tense Past: Cultural Essays in Trauma and Memory*. New York, London: Routledge, 1996.
4. Austin, Allan E. *Elizabeth Bowen*. New York: Twayne Publishers, 1971.
5. Bachelard, Gaston. *The Poetics of Space*. Boston: Beacon Press, 1994.
6. Bakhtin, M. M., Holquist, Michael. *The Dialogic Imagination: Four Essays*. Austin: University of Texas Press, 1981.
7. Boehmer, Elleke. *Colonial and Postcolonial Literature*. Oxford University Press, 2005.
8. Bence-Jones, Mark. *A Guide to Irish Country Houses*. London: Constable, 1996.
9. Benjamin, Walter. *The Arcades Project*. Trans. Howard Eiland and Kevin McLaughlin. Cambridge, MA: Harvard University Press, 1999.
10. Bennett, Andrew and Royle, Nicholas. *Elizabeth Bowen and the Dissolution of the Novel: Still Lives*. New York: St. Martin's Press, 1995.
11. Bernal, J. D. *The World, the Flesh & the Devil: An Enquiry into the Future of the Three Enemies of the Rational Soul*. [Online] http://vserver1.cscs.lsa.umich.edu/~crshalizi/Bernal [Accessed 8 Aug. 2013]
12. Blodgett, Harriet. *Patterns of Reality: Elizabeth Bowen's Novels*. The Hague: Mouton, 1975.
13. Bloom, Harold, ed. *Bloom's Literary Themes: Alienation*. New York: Bloom's Literary Criticism, 2009.
14. Bloom, William. *Personal Identity, National Identity and International Relations*. Cambridge University Press, 1993.
15. Bowen, Elizabeth. *Afterthought. Pieces about Writing*. London: Longmans, 1962.
16. Bowen, Elizabeth. *The Bazaar and Other Stories*. Ed. Allan Hepburn. Edinburgh University Press, 2008.
17. Bowen, Elizabeth. "The Big House". *Collected Impressions*. London: Longmans Green, 1950. 195–200.
18. Bowen, Elizabeth. *Bowen's Court and Seven Winters*. London: Vintage, 1999.
19. Bowen, Elizabeth. *The Collected Stories of Elizabeth Bowen*. New York: Vintage Books, 1982.

20. Bowen, Elizabeth. *The Death of the Heart* (1938). London: Penguin Books, 1962.
21. Bowen Elizabeth *The House in Paris* (1935). London: Penguin Books, 1987.
22. Bowen, Elizabeth. *The Last September* (1929). New York: Anchor Books, 2000.
23. Bowen, Elizabeth. *People, Places, Things*. Ed. Allan Hepburn. Edinburgh University Press, 2008.
24. Bowen, Elizabeth. "Pictures and Conversations" (1975). *The Literature of the Irish in Britain: Autobiography and Memoir, 1725-2001*. Ed. Liam Harte. London: Palgrave Macmillan, 2009. 125-28.
25. Bowen, Elizabeth. *A World of Love* (1955). London: Penguin Twentieth Century Classics. 1993.
26. Bradbury, Malcolm. *The Modern British Novel*. London: Penguin Books, 2001.
27. Brezinka, Wolfgang. *Socialization and Education: Essays in Conceptual Criticism*. Transl. James Stuart Brice. Westport: Greenwood Publishing Group, 1994.
28. Brooke, Jocelyn. *Elizabeth Bowen*. London: Longmans, 1952.
29. Brown, Bill. *A Sense of Things: The Object Matter of American Literature*. Chicago and London: The University of Chicago Press, 2003.
30. Carpenter, Andrew. "Double Vision in Anglo-Irish Literature". *Place, Personality and the Irish Writer*. Ed. Andrew Carpenter. Gerrards Cross: Colin Smythe, 1977. 173-89.
31. Caruth, Cathy. "Trauma and Experience: Introduction". *Trauma: Explorations in Memory*. Ed. Cathy Caruth. Baltimore: Johns Hopkins University Press, 1995. 3-12.
32. Caruth, Cathy. *Unclaimed Experience: Trauma, Narrative, and History*. Baltimore: Johns Hopkins University Press, 1996.
33. Castle, Terry. *The Female Thermometer: Eighteenth-Century Culture and the Invention of the Uncanny*. New York and Oxford: Oxford University Press, 1994.
34. Chafin, Bethany. *Created Spaces: Domestic Myth-making in the Novels of Elizabeth Bowen*. Winston-Salem: Wake Forest University Graduate School of Arts and Sciences, 2011.
35. Chessman, Hariett S. "Women and Language in the Fiction of Elizabeth Bowen". *Twentieth Century Literature* 29.1 (Spring 1983): 69-85.
36. Christensen, Lis. *Elizabeth Bowen: The Later Fiction*. Copenhagen: Museum Tusculanum Press, 2001.

37. Cirlot, J. C. *Dictionary of Symbols*. Routledge, 2002.
38. Coates, John. "The Moral Argument of Elizabeth Bowen's Ghost Stories". *Renascence: Essays on Values in Literature* 52.4 (2000): 293–309.
39. Collins, Jo and Jervis, John. "Introduction". *Uncanny Modernity: Cultural Theories, Modern Anxieties*. Ed. Jo Collins and John Jervis. Basingstoke and New York: Palgrave Macmillan, 2008. 1–9.
40. Connon, Daisy. *Subjects Not-at-home: Forms of the Uncanny in the Contemporary French Novel*. Amsterdam, New York: Rodopi, 2010.
41. Corcoran, Neil. *Elizabeth Bowen: The Enforced Return*. Oxford: Clarendon Press, 2004.
42. Coulson, Victoria. "Elizabeth Bowen". *The Cambridge Companion to English Novelists*. Ed. Adrian Poole. Cambridge University Press, 2009. 377–92.
43. Craig, Patricia. *Elizabeth Bowen*. Harmondsworth: Penguin Books, 1986.
44. Creed, Barbara. *Phallic Panic: Film, Horror and the Primal Uncanny*. Melbourne University Press, 2005.
45. Crowell, Ellen. "Ghosting the Llangollen Ladies: Female Intimacies, Ascendancy Exiles, and the Anglo-Irish Novel". *Eire-Ireland* 39.3 (2004): 202–27.
46. D'Alton, Ian. *The Last Big House: perspectives from Lennox Robinson and Elizabeth Bowen*. A paper read to the Royal Irish Academy conference "The Big House in Twentieth Century Irish Writing", Dublin 14–15 October 2008 [Online] http://independent.academia.edu/IandAlton/Papers/705295/The_Last_Big_House_perspectives_from_Lennox_Robinson_and_Elizabeth_Bowen [Accessed 6 Dec. 2011].
47. Deane, Seamus. *Celtic Revivals: Essays in Modern Irish Literature 1880–1980*. London and Boston: Faber and Faber, 1985.
48. Derrida, Jacques. *Specters of Marks*. New York, London: Routledge, 2006.
49. D'hoker, Elke. "The Poetics of House and Home in the Short Stories of Elizabeth Bowen". *Orbis Litterarum* 67:4 (2012): 267–89.
50. DiBattista, Maria. "Elizabeth Bowen and the Maternal Sublime". *Troubled Legacies: Narrative and Inheritance*. Ed. Allan Hepburn. University of Toronto Press, 2007. 219–38.
51. Doan, Laura. "'Woman's Place *Is* the Home': Conservative Sapphic Modernity". *Sapphic Modernities: Sexuality, Women and National Culture*. Ed. Laura Doan and Jane Garrity. New York: Palgrave Macmillan, 2006. 91–107.
52. Donnelly, Brian. "The Big House in the Recent Novel". *Studies: An Irish Quarterly Review* 64 (Summer 1975): 133–42.

53. Drewery, Claire. *Modernist Short Fiction by Women: The Liminal in Katherine Mansfield, Dorothy Richardson, May Sinclair and Virginia Wolf.* Farnham: Ashgate, 2011.
54. Dukes, Thomas. "The Unorthodox Plots of Elizabeth Bowen". *Studies in the Humanities* 16.1 (1989): 10–23.
55. Eckhard, Petra. *Chronotopes of the Uncanny. Time and Space in Postmodern New York Novels. Paul Auster's "City of Glass" and Toni Morrison's "Jazz".* Bielefeld: Transcript Verlag, 2011.
56. Edgar, Andrew. "The Uncanny, Alienation and Strangeness: The Entwining of Political and Medical Metaphor". *Medicine, Health Care, and Philosophy* 14.3 (2011): 313–22.
57. Ellison, David. *Ethics and Aesthetics in European Modernist Literature: From the Sublime to the Uncanny.* Cambridge University Press, 2004.
58. Ellmann, Maud. *The Shadow Across the Page.* Edinburgh University Press, 2003.
59. Felman, Shoshana and Laub, Dori. *Testimony: Crises of Witnessing in Literature, Psychoanalysis, and History.* New York, London: Routledge, 1992.
60. Ferber, Michael. *A Dictionary of Literary Symbols.* New York and Cambridge: Cambridge University Press, 1999.
61. Foster, Roy. "Irish and Regional: Locale in Elizabeth Bowen's Writing". *Elizabeth Bowen Remembered: The Farahy Addresses.* Ed. Eibhear Walshe. Dublin: Four Courts Press, 1998. 21–7.
62. Foster, R.F. "Prints on the Scene: Elizabeth Bowen and the Landscape of Childhood". *The Irish Story: Telling Tales and Making It Up in Ireland.* Oxford University Press, 2002. 148–63.
63. Foucault, Michel. *Of Other Spaces, Heterotopias* (1967) [Online]. www.foucault.info/documents/heteroTopia/foucault.heteroTopia.en.html [Accessed 17 Oct. 2012].
64. Freedman, Ariela. *Death, Men, and Modernism: Trauma and Narrative in British Fiction from Hardy to Woolf.* New York and London: Routledge, 2003.
65. Freud, Sigmund. *Beyond the Pleasure Principle* (1922). Ed. Todd Dufresne. Transl. Gregory C. Richter. Toronto: Broadview Editions, 2011.
66. Freud, Sigmund. "Creative Writers and Day-Dreaming" (1908). *20th Century Criticism.* Ed. David Lodge. London: Longman, 1972. 36–42.
67. Freud, Sigmund. *A General Introduction to Psychoanalysis* (1920). New York: Boni and Liveright, Bartleby.com, 2010. [Online] www.bartleby.com/283/ [Accessed 4 Jan. 2013].

68. Freud, Sigmund. *The Interpretation of Dreams*. Trans. A. A. Brill. New York: Modern Library, 1950.
69. Freud, Sigmund. "Remarks on the Theory and Practice of Dream-Interpretation" (1923). *The Standard Edition of the Complete Psychological Works of Sigmund Freud*. Trans. James Strachey. *Volume XIX (1923–1925): The Ego and the Id and Other Works*. Vintage Classics, 2001. 107–22.
70. Freud, Sigmund. "Remembering, Repeating and Working-Through" (1914). [Online] http://www.newschool.edu/tcds/krakow/KR08MEM/Session3/Sigmund%20Freud%20-%20Remembering,%20Repeating%20and%20Working-Through.pdf [Accessed 25 Oct. 2012].
71. *Freud, Sigmund. Selected Writings. Ed. Robert Coles. Trans. James Strachey. New York: Book-of-the-Month Club, 1997.*
72. Freud, Sigmund. "The 'Uncanny'". *The Standard Edition of the Complete Psychological Works of Sigmund Freud*. Trans. James Strachey, with Anna Freud, Alix Strachey and Alan Tyson. *Volume XVII (1917–1919): An Infantile Neurosis and Other Works*. London: Hogarth Press and the Institute of Psycho-Analysis, 1986. 217–256.
73. Frost, Brian J. *The Essential Guide to Werewolf Literature*. Madison, London: Popular Press, 2003.
74. Genet, Jacqueline, ed. *The Big House in Ireland: Reality and Representation*. Dingle: Rowman & Littlefield, 1991.
75. Gilbert, Paul. "The Idea of a National Literature". *Literature and the Political Imagination*. Ed. John Horton and Andrea T. Baumeister. London and New York: Routledge, 2003. 198–217.
76. Gill, Richard. "The Country House in a Time of Toubles". *Elizabeth Bowen: Modern Critical Views*. Ed. Harold Bloom. New York: Chelsea House Publishers, 1987. 51–61.
77. Gillies, Mary Ann. *Henri Bergson and British Modernism*. Montreal, Kingston: McGill-Queen's Press, 1996.
78. *Gillis, J. R. For Better, for Worse: British Marriages, 1600 to the Present. Oxford University Press, 1985.*
79. Giora, Zvi. *The Unconscious and its Narratives. Psychoanalytic Crosscurrents Series*. New York University Press, 1992.
80. Glendinning, Victoria. "Gardens and Gardening in the Writings of Elizabeth Bowen". *Elizabeth Bowen: Modern Critical Views*. Ed. Harold Bloom. New York: Chelsea House Publishers, 1987. 28–34.
81. Bomarito, Jessica, ed. *Gothic Literature: A Gale Critical Companion*. Vol. 3. Farmington Hills, Mich.: Thomson Gale, 2006.

82. Hachey, Thomas E. and McCaffrey, Lawrence John. *The Irish Experience Since 1800: A Concise History*. New York and London: M.E. Sharpe, 2010.
83. Hand, Derek. "Ghosts from Our Future: Bowen and the Unfinished Business of Living". *Elizabeth Bowen*. Ed. Eibhear Walshe. Dublin: Irish Academic Press, 2009. 65–76.
84. Hanson, Clare. *Hysterical Fictions: The 'Woman's Novel' in the Twentieth Century*. London: Palgrave Macmillan, 2000.
85. Hartnett, Anthony. *A sense of Place in the Fiction of Elizabeth Bowen*. MA thesis. University College, Cork, 1983.
86. Heidegger, Martin. *Being and Time*. State University of New York Press, 1996.
87. Heijnen, Adriënne and Edgar, Iain. "Imprints of Dreaming". *History and Anthropology* 21.3 (September 2010): 217–26.
88. Henn, Thomas Rice. *Last Essays*. Gerrards Cross: Colin Smythe, 1976.
89. Hepburn, Allan. *Enchanted Objects: Visual Art in Contemporary Fiction*. University of Toronto Press, 2010a.
90. Hepburn, Allan, ed. *Listening in: Broadcasts, Speeches, and Interviews by Elizabeth Bowen*. Edinburgh University Press, 2010b.
91. Herman, Judith. *Trauma and Recovery*. New York: Basic Books, 1992.
92. Hinrichs, Martina. *Negativität als Struktur: eine Untersuchung ausgewählter Romane und Kurzgeschichten von Elizabeth Bowen*. Diss. Universität Hannover, 1998.
93. Holdsworth, Angela. *Out of the Doll's House: The Story of Women in the Twentieth Century*. London: BBC Books, 1988.
94. Holland, Norman N. "Foreword: The Literarity of Dreams, the Dreaminess of Literature". *The Dream and the Text: Essays on Literature and Language*. Ed. Carol Schreier Rupprecht. State University of New York Press, 1993. ix-xx.
95. Hughes, Douglas A. "Cracks in the Psyche: Elizabeth Bowen's *The Demon Lover*". *Studies in Short Fiction* 10 (1973): 411–3.
96. Gildersleeve, Jessica. *Elizabeth Bowen and the Writing of Trauma*. PhD thesis. University of Bristol, 2009.
97. Inglesby, Elizabeth C. "'Expressive Objects': Elizabeth Bowen's Narrative Materializes". *Modern Fiction Studies* 53.2 (Summer 2007): 306–33.
98. Ingman, Heather. *Twentieth-century Fiction by Irish Women: Nation and Gender*. Aldershot: Ashgate Publishing, 2007.
99. Jentsch, Ernst. "On the Psychology of the Uncanny". *Angelaki: a new journal in philosophy, literature, and the social sciences* 2.1 (1996): 7–16.

100. Jervis, John. "Uncanny Presences". *Uncanny Modernity: Cultural Theories, Modern Anxieties*. Ed. Jo Collins and John Jervis. Basingstoke and New York: Palgrave Macmillan, 2008. 10–50.
101. Johnson, Kathryn. "'Phantasmagoric Hinterlands': Adolescence and Anglo-Ireland in Elizabeth Bowen's *The House in Paris* and the *Death of the Heart*". *Irish Women Writers: New Critical Perspectives*. Ed. Elke D'hoker, Raphael Ingelbien and Hedwig Schwall. Oxford, Bern and Berlin: Peter Lang, 2011. 207–25.
102. Johnson, Laurie Ruth. *Aesthetic Anxiety: Uncanny Symptoms in German Literature and Culture*. Amsterdam: Rodopi, 2010.
103. Johnson, Sandra H. *The Space Between: Literary Epiphany in the Work of Annie Dillard*. The Kent State University Press, 1992.
104. Kenney, Edwin J. *Elizabeth Bowen*. Lewisburg: Bucknell University Press, London: Associated University Presses, 1975.
105. Kent, Susan. *Sex and Suffrage in Britain 1860-1914*. Princeton University Press, 1990.
106. Kershner, R. B. *The Twentieth-Century Novel: An Introduction*. Boston and New York: Bedford Books, 1997.
107. Kędra-Kardela, Anna. "Boundary-Crossing in Elizabeth Bowen's Short Story 'The Happy Autumn Fields'". *Dangerous Crossing: Papers on Transgression in Literature and Culture*. Ed. Monica Loeb and Gerald Porter. Umeå University, 1999. 177–85.
108. Kędra-Kardela, Anna. "The Literary Work and Its Reader. A Narratological Analysis of Elizabeth Bowen's 'The Cheery Soul'". *Perspectives On Literature And Culture*. Ed. Leszek S. Kolek, Aleksandra Kędzierska and Anna Kędra-Kardela. Lublin: Wydawnictwo Marii Curie-Skłodowskiej, 2004.101–9.
109. Kędra-Kardela, Anna. "The Narrator, the Narratee and the Reader in Elizabeth Bowen's Short Stories "Pink May" and 'Careless Talk'". *Texts of Literature. Texts of Culture*. Ed. Ludmiła Gruszewska Blaim and Artur Blaim. Lublin: Wydawnictwo Marii Curie-Skłodowskiej, 2005. 193–205.
110. Kiberd, Declan. *Inventing Ireland: The Literature of the Modern Nation*. London: Vintage, 1996.
111. Kihlstrom, John F. "Suffering from Reminiscences: Exhumed Memory, Implicit Memory and the Return of the Repressed". *Recovered Memories and False Memories*. Ed. M. A. Conway. Oxford University Press, 1997. 100–17.
112. Kitagawa, Yoriko. "Anticipating the Postmodern Self: Elizabeth Bowen's *The Death of the Heart*". *English Studies* 81: 5 (2000): 484–96.

113. Kovacs, Lee. *The Haunted Screen: Ghosts in Literature and Film*. Jefferson, NC: McFarland, 2005.
114. Kramer, Milton. "Dream Translation: An Approach to Understanding Dreams". *New Directions in Dream Interpretation*. Ed. Gayle Delaney. State University of New York Press, 1993. 155–94.
115. Kreilkamp, Vera. *The Anglo-Irish Novel and the Big House*. New York: Syracuse University Press, 1998.
116. Kreilkamp, Vera. "Bowen: Ascendancy Modernist". *Elizabeth Bowen*. Ed. Eibhear Walshe. Dublin: Irish Academic Press, 2009. 12–26.
117. Kreilkamp, Vera. "The Novel of the Big House". *The Cambridge Companion to the Irish Novel*. Ed. John Wilson Foster. Cambridge University Press, 2006. 60–77.
118. Kristeva, Julia. *Proust and the Sense of Time*. New York: Columbia University Press, 1993.
119. Kühn-Rudenko, Kateryna. *The Uncanny Narrated: Functions of Narrative Stratagies in Different Types of Uncanny Representations in Stephen King's Novels It and Firestarter*. Trier: Wissenschaftlicher Verlag Trier, 2011.
120. Lacan, Jacques. *Le Séminaire. Livre VIII. Le Transfert. 1960–61*. Ed. Jacques-Alain Miller. Paris: Seuil, 1991.
121. Lacan, Jacques. *The Seminar. Book I. Freud's Papers on Technique* (1953–54). Trans. John Forrester. New York: Norton, 1988.
122. Langbaum, Robert. "The Epiphanic Mode in Wordsworth and Modern Literature. Moments of Moment". *Aspects of the Literary Epiphany*. Ed. Wim Tigges. Amsterdam and Atlanta, GA: Rodopi, 1999. 37–84.
123. Lavlinski, D. V. Rasskazy Elizabeth Bowen (literaturnyj kontekst i osobennosti poetiki) [russ.]. Diss. Voronezh, 2011. (Лавлинский Д. В. Рассказы Элизабет Боуэн (литературный контекст и особенности поэтики). Дисс. кандид. филол. наук. Воронеж, 2011.)
124. Lawley, Alanna. *A sense of the Uncanny within domestic space*. [Online] http://www.alannalawley.com/writings/Alanna-Lawley-Domestic-Space.pdf [Accessed 29 Sep. 2012].
125. Lee, Hermione. *Elizabeth Bowen: An Estimation*. London: Vision; Totowa, NJ: Barnes, 1981.
126. Lotman, Jurij. *The Structure of Artistic Text*. Trans. Ronald Vroon, Ann Arbor. University of Michigan Press, 1977.
127. Lubbers, Klaus. "Continuity and Change in Irish Fiction: The Case of the Big-House Novel". *Ancestral Voices: The Big House in Anglo-Irish Literature*. Ed. Otto Rauchbauer. Dublin: The Lilliput Press, 1992. 17–29.

128. Luckhurst, Roger. "The Uncanny After Freud: The Contemporary Trauma Subject and the Fiction of Stephen King". *Uncanny Modernity: Cultural Theories, Modern Anxieties*. Ed. Jo Collins and John Jervis. Basingstoke and New York: Palgrave Macmillan, 2008. 128–45.
129. Magot, Céline. "Prosthetic Goddesses: Ambiguous Identities in the Age of Speed". *Textual Practice* 27.1 (2013): 127–42.
130. Malcolm, David and Malcolm, Cheryl Alexander. *A Companion to the British and Irish Short Story*. Chichester, UK: Wiley-Blackwell, 2008.
131. Matz, Jesse. *The Modern Novel*. Oxford: Blackwell, 2004.
132. McCarthy, Thomas. "Introduction". *Bowen's Court* by Elizabeth Bowen. Cork: The Collins Press, 1998. ix-xvi.
133. McCormack, William John. *Ascendancy and Tradition in Anglo-Irish Literary History from 1789 to 1939*. Oxford: Clarendon Press, 1985.
134. McGowan, Martha. "The Enclosed Garden in Elizabeth Bowen's *A World of Love*". *Eire-Ireland. A Journal of Irish Studies* 16.1 (1981): 55–70.
135. Medoff, Jeslyn. "'There Is No Elsewhere': Elizabeth Bowen's Perceptions of War". *Modern Fiction Studies* 30.1 (Spring 1984): 73–81.
136. Menczer, Katy Alexandra. *From Flesh to Fiction: The Visible and the Invisible in the work of Maurice Merleau-Ponty, Eudora Welty and Elizabeth Bowen*. PhD thesis. Queen Mary, University of London, 2006.
137. Miller, Brook, et al. "Narrative, Meaning and Agency in *The Heat of the Day*". *Elizabeth Bowen: New Critical Perspectives*. Ed. Susan Osborn. Cork University Press, 2009. 132–48.
138. Miller, Marlowe A. *Masterpieces of British Modernism*. Westport and London: Greenwood Press, 2006.
139. Millet, Kate. "The Debate over Women: Ruskin vs. Mill". *Suffer and Be Still: Women in the Victorian Age*. Ed. M. Vicinus. Bloomington: Indiana University Press, 1973.
140. Mitchel, Juliet and Rose, Jacqueline, eds. *Feminine Sexuality: Jacque Lacan and the École Freudienne*. London: Macmillan, 1982.
141. Morgan, Pauline. *A World of Ghosts*. PhD thesis. University of Sussex, 2003.
142. Nalbantian, Suzanne. *Memory in Literature*. London: Palgrave Macmillan, 2003.
143. Nycz, Ryszard. *Literatura jako trop rzeczywistości: poetyka epifanii w nowoczesnej literaturze polskiej*. Kraków: Universitas, 2001.
144. Obeyesekere, Gananath. *The Work of Culture: Symbolic Transformation in Psychoanalysis and Anthropology*. University of Chicago Press, 1990.

145. O'Connor, Marcella. *Time in Elizabeth Bowen's Irish Fiction*. MA thesis. National University of Ireland, Cork. 2011.
146. O'Tool, Tina. "Ungenerate Spirits: The Counter-Cultural Experiments of George Egerton and Elizabeth Bowen". *Irish Women Writers: New Critical Perspectives*. Ed. Elke D'hoker, Raphael Ingelbien and Hedwig Schwall. Oxford, Bern and Berlin: Peter Lang, 2011. 227–244.
147. Otten, Charlotte F., ed. *The Literary Werewolf: An Anthology*. New York: Syracuse University Press, 2002.
148. Palko, Abigail. "Colonial Modernism's Thwarted Maternity: Elizabeth Bowen's *The House in Paris* and Jean Rhy's *Voyage in the Dark*". *Textual Practice* 27.1 (2013): 89–108.
149. Palmer, Paulina. *The Queer Uncanny*. Cardiff: University of Wales Press, 2012.
150. Parkin, Alan J. *Memory and Amnesia: An Introduction*. Oxford: Basil Blakcwell, 1987.
151. Parsons, Deborah L. "Souls Astray: Elizabeth Bowen's Landscape of War". *Women: A Cultural Review* 8.1 (1997): 24–32.
152. Peel, Ellen. "Psychoanalysis and the Uncanny". *Comparative Literature Studies* 17.4 *Proceedings of the Second Northeast Student Conference Held at Pennsylvania State University*, April 7–8, 1979 (Dec., 1980): 410–7.
153. Pennartz, Paul J. J. "Home: The Experience of Atmosphere". *At Home: An Anthropology of Domestic Space*. Ed. Irene Cieraad. New York: Syracuse University Press, 2006. 95–106.
154. Poincaré, Henri. *Science and Hypothesis* (1905). Trans. W. J. Greenstreet. New York: Cosimo, 2007.
155. Powell, Kersti Tarien. *Irish Fiction: An Introduction*. New York: Continuum International Publishing Group, 2004.
156. Rauchbauer, Otto. "Introduction", "The Big House and Irish History: An Introductory Sketch" and "The Big House in the Irish Short Story after 1918: A Critical Survey". *Ancestral Voices: The Big House in Anglo-Irish Literature*. Ed. Otto Rauchbauer. Dublin: The Lilliput Press, 1992. vii-x, 1–15, 159–93.
157. Ridge, Emily. "Elizabeth Bowen, Howards End and the Luggage of Modernity". *Textual Practice* 27.1 (2013): 109–26.
158. Rose, Jacqueline. "Bizarre Objects: Mary Butts and Elizabeth Bowen". *Critical Quarterly* 42.1 (2000): 75–85.
159. Roth, Michael S. *Memory, Trauma, and History: Essays on Living with the Past*. New York: Columbia University Press, 2013.
160. Royle, Nicholas. *Jacques Derrida*. London and New York: Routledge, 2003a.

161. Royle, Nicholas. *The Uncanny*. Manchester University Press, 2003b.
162. Royle, Nicholas. *Veering: A Theory of Literature*. Edinburgh University Press, 2011.
163. Saler, Michael. "Profane Illuminations, Delicate and Mysterious Flames: Mass Culture and Uncanny Gnosis". *Uncanny Modernity: Cultural Theories, Modern Anxieties*. Ed. Jo Collins and John Jervis. Basingstoke and New York: Palgrave Macmillan, 2008. 181–200.
164. Smith, Anthony D. *National Identity*. Reno: University of Nevada Press, 1993.
165. States, Bert O. "Bizarreness in Dreams and Other Fictions". *The Dream and the Text: Essays on Literature and Language*. Ed. Carol Schreier Rupprecht. State University of New York Press, 1993. 13–31.
166. Steveker, Lena. *Identity and Cultural Memory in the Fiction of A. S. Byatt*. London: Palgrave Macmillan, 2009.
167. Stewart, Victoria. *Narratives of Memory. British Writing of the 1940s*. London: Palgrave Macmillan, 2006.
168. Tatar, Maria M. "The Houses of Fiction: Toward a Definition of the Uncanny". *Comparative Literature* 33.2 (Spring, 1981): 167–82.
169. Taylor, Charles. *Sources of the Self: The Making of the Modern Identity*. Cambridge University Press, 2006.
170. Thurston, Luke. "Double-crossing: Elizabeth Bowen's ghostly short fiction". *Textual Practice* 27.1 (2013): 7–28.
171. Thurston, Luke. *Literary Ghosts from the Victorians to Modernism: The Haunting Interval*. New York: Routledge, 2012.
172. Todorov, Tzvetan. *The Fantastic: A Structural Approach to a Literary Genre*. Cornell University Press, 1975.
173. Torrijos, Esther Rey. *La Narrative de Elizabeth Bowen: Estudio de Aspectos Culturales y Formales*. Diss. Universidad Complutense de Madrid, 2004.
174. Towheed, Shafquat. "Territory, space, modernity: Elizabeth Bowen's *The Demon Lover and Other Stories* and Wartime London". *Elizabeth Bowen: New Critical Perspectives*. Ed. Susan Osborn. Cork University Press, 2009. 113–31.
175. Trigg, Dylan. *The Memory of Place: A Phenomenology of the Uncanny*. Athens: Ohio University Press, 2012.
176. Vidler, Anthony. *The Architectural Uncanny*. Cambridge, Mass.: MIT Press, 1994.
177. Walsh, Keri. "Elizabeth Bowen, Surrealist". *Éire-Ireland: A Journal of Irish Studies*, 42.3–4 (Fall-Winter 2007): 126–47.

178. Walshe, Eibhear. *Elizabeth Bowen*. Dublin and Portland: Irish Academic Press, 2009.
179. Wasson, Sara. *Urban Gothic of the Second World War. Dark London*. Basingstoke: Palgrave Macmillan, 2010.
180. Weekes, Ann Owens. *Irish Women Writers: An Uncharted Tradition*. Lexington: University Press of Kentucky, 1990.
181. Weekes, Ann Owens. "Women Novelists, 1930s-1960s". *The Cambridge Companion to the Irish Novel*. Ed. John Wilson Foster. Cambridge University Press, 2006. 189–204.
182. Wells-Lassagne, Shannon. "'He Believed in Empire'. Colonial Concerns in Elizabeth Bowen's *The Last September*". *Irish Studies Review* 15.4 (2007): 451–63.
183. Welty, Eudora. *A Writer's Eye: Collected Book Reviews*. Ed. Pearl Amelia McHaney. Jackson: University Press of Mississippi, 1994.
184. Whitehead, Anna. *Trauma Fiction*. Edinburgh University Press, 2004.
185. Wightman, Beth. "Geopolitics and the Sight of the Nation: Elizabeth Bowen's *The Last September*". *Literature Interpretation Theory* 18.1 (2007): 37–64.
186. Williams, Melanie. *Empty Justice: One Hundred Years of Law, Literature and Philosophy*. London and Sydney: Cavendish Publishing Limited, 2002.
187. Wolfreys, Julian. "The Urban Uncanny: The City, the Subject, and Ghostly Modernity". *Uncanny Modernity: Cultural Theories, Modern Anxieties*. Ed. Jo Collins and John Jervis. Basingstoke and New York: Palgrave Macmillan, 2008. 168–80.
188. Wolfreys, Julian. *Writing London: the trace of the urban text from Blake to Dickens*. Houndmills, UK: Palgrave Macmillan, 1998.
189. Wurtz, James F. "Elizabeth Bowen, Modernism, and the Spectre of Anglo-Ireland". *Estudios Irlandeses* 5 (2010): 119–28.
190. Zweiniger-Bargielowska, Ina, ed. *Women in twentieth-century Britain*. Harlow: Longman, 2001.

Index

A
Abrams, M. H. 25
Adams, Timothy Dow 55
Antze, Paul 63, 84
Austin, Allan E. 52, 122

B
Bachelard, Gaston 12, 28, 29, 40, 68, 81, 82
Bakhtin, M. M. 24
Bence-Jones, Mark 94
Benjamin, Walter 26, 30
Bennett, Andrew 23, 72, 84, 109, 112, 120, 121
Bergson, Henri 21, 49
Bernal, J. D. 74
Blodgett, Harriet 96
Bloom, Harold 23
Bloom, William 33
Boehmer, Elleke 32
Bomarito, Jessica 20
Bradbury, Malcolm 21, 39
Brezinka, Wolfgang 77
Brooke, Jocelyn 53, 65, 67, 82
Brown, Bill 67, 77

C
Carpenter, Andrew 107, 108, 116
Caruth, Cathy 35, 37, 52
Castle, Terry 20, 35, 111
Chafin, Bethany 11, 39, 41
Chessman, Hariett S. 65, 79
Christensen, Lis 102
Coates, John 44, 75
Collins, Jo 19, 22, 31
Connon, Daisy 40, 41, 107
Conrad, Joseph 24
Corcoran, Neil 11, 105

Craig, Patricia 56
Creed, Barbara 110
Crowell, Ellen 56

D
D'Alton, Ian 95
Dante 53
Deane, Seamus 107
Derrida, Jacques 19
D'hoker, Elke 40, 41, 59, 60
DiBattista, Maria 53
Doan, Laura 57
Drewery, Claire 39
Dukes, Thomas 79

E
Eckhard, Petra 26, 50
Edgar, Andrew 22
Edgar, Iain 81
Edgeworth, Maria 95
Ellison, David 20, 23
Ellmann, Maud 11

F
Felman, Shoshana 36
Ferber, Michael 46
Foster, Roy 72, 75, 109
Foucault, Michel 12, 24, 25, 26
France, Anatole 43, 52
Freedman, Ariela 13
Freud, Sigmund 5, 12–25, 28, 29, 34, 36, 52, 64, 67, 79–82, 120, 125
Frost, Brian J. 87

G
Genet, Jacqueline 112, 114, 121
Gide, André 20
Gilbert, Paul 95, 112, 113

Gildersleeve, Jessica 11
Gill, Richard 94, 95
Gillies, Mary Ann 49
Gillis, J. R. 56
Giora, Zvi 82
Glendinning, Victoria 51

H
Hachey, Thomas E. 98
Hand, Derek 116
Hanson, Clare 78
Hartnett, Anthony 107
Heidegger, Martin 12, 18
Heijnen, Adriënne 81
Henn, Thomas Rice 94
Hepburn, Allan 41, 47, 48, 57
Herman, Judith 35
Hinrichs, Martina 56
Hoffmann, E. T. A. 16
Holdsworth, Angela 56
Holland, Norman N. 83
Holquist, Michael 127
Hughes, Douglas A. 117

I
Inglesby, Elizabeth C. 30
Ingman, Heather 78

J
Jentsch, Ernst 5, 12, 15, 16, 18, 22, 23, 73
Jervis, John 19, 22, 24, 25, 27
Johnson, Kathryn 75
Johnson, Laurie Ruth 18
Johnson, Sandra H. 51
Joyce, James 11, 21

K
Kafka, Franz 20
Kenney, Edwin J. 51–53, 73, 108, 116
Kent, Susan 61
Kershner, R. B. 21, 39

Kędra-Kardela, Anna 11, 120
Kiberd, Declan 96
Kihlstrom, John F. 80
Kitagawa, Yoriko 73–74
Kovacs, Lee 112
Kramer, Milton 82
Kreilkamp, Vera 11, 39, 61, 93–95, 104, 113, 116
Kristeva, Julia 52
Kühn-Rudenko, Kateryna 37

L
Lacan, Jacques 48, 119, 120
Lambek, Michael 63, 84
Langbaum, Robert 25
Lavlinski, D. V. 11
Lawley, Alanna 27, 34
Lee, Hermione 109, 116
Le Fanu, Sheridan 95, 100
Lotman, Jurij 30, 70, 120
Lubbers, Klaus 93, 94
Luckhurst, Roger 34

M
Magot, Céline 47
Malcolm, Cheryl Alexander 95, 96
Malcolm, David 95, 96
Maturin, Charles Robert 95
Matz, Jesse 20
McCarthy, Thomas 11
McCormack, William John 94
McGowan, Martha 118
Medoff, Jeslyn 95
Menczer, Katy Alexandra 11
Miller, Brook 41
Miller, Marlowe A. 21
Millet, Kate 56
Mitchel, Juliet 119
Morgan, Pauline 11

N
Nycz, Ryszard 25

O
Obeyesekere, Gananath 83
O'Connor, Marcella 111, 114, 119
O'Tool, Tina 78
Otten, Charlotte F. 87

P
Palko, Abigail 53
Palmer, Paulina 31, 32, 35, 52, 110
Parkin, Alan J. 117
Parsons, Deborah L. 40, 99
Peel, Ellen 16
Pennartz, Paul J. J. 40
Poe, Alan 100
Poincaré, Henri 30, 33
Powell, Kersti Tarien 94, 95
Proust, Marcel 20, 21 49, 52

R
Rauchbauer, Otto 93, 94, 112
Ricoeur, Paul 83
Ridge, Emily 43, 75
Rose, Jacqueline 45, 119
Roth, Michael S. 63
Royle, Nicholas 12, 18, 21, 23, 36, 37, 39, 41, 47, 48, 52, 55, 72, 74, 84, 109, 112

S
Saler, Michael 31
Schelling, Friedrich 25
Smith, Anthony D. 32
States, Bert O. 85

Steveker, Lena 33, 49
Stewart, Victoria 35, 49

T
Tatar, Maria M. 21, 118
Taylor, Charles 31
Thurston, Luke 11, 86, 115
Todorov, Tzvetan 119
Torrijos, Esther Rey 11, 77
Towheed, Shafquat 40
Trigg, Dylan 33, 40, 52, 63, 81

V
Vidler, Anthony 20, 26, 27, 29

W
Walsh, Keri 83
Walshe, Eibhear 11, 102
Wasson, Sara 40, 35, 36, 52
Weekes, Ann Owens 96, 114
Wells-Lassagne, Shannon 97
Welty, Eudora 83
Whitehead, Anna 34, 36, 114
Whitman, Walt 31
Wightman, Beth 97
Williams, Melanie 44
Wolfreys, Julian 23, 26, 27
Woolf, Virginia 11, 20, 21
Wurtz, James F. 112, 113

Z
Zweiniger-Bargielowska, Ina 56

Mediated Fictions

Studies in Verbal and Visual Narratives

Series Editors: Artur Blaim and Ludmiła Gruszewska-Blaim

Vol. 1 Katarzyna Pisarska: Mediating the World in the Novels of Iain Banks. The Paradigms of Fiction. 2013.

Vol. 2 Anna Kędra-Kardela and Andrzej Sławomir Kowalczyk (eds.): Expanding the Gothic Canon. Studies in Literature, Film and New Media. 2014.

Vol. 3 Grzegorz Czemiel: Limits of Orality and Textuality in Ciaran Carson's Poetry. 2014.

Vol. 4 Artur Blaim and Ludmiła Gruszewska-Blaim (eds.): Mediated Utopias: From Literature to Cinema. 2015.

Vol. 5 Justyna Laura Galant: *Painted Devils, Siren Tongues*. The Semiotic Universe of Jacobean Tragedy. 2015.

Vol. 6 Marta Komsta: Welcome to the Chemical Theatre. The Urban Chronotope in Peter Ackroyd´s Fiction. 2015.

Vol. 7 Urszula Terentowicz-Fotyga: Dreams, Nightmares and Empty Signifiers. The English Country House in the Contemporary Novel. 2015.

Vol. 8 Barbara Klonowska / Zofia Kolbuszewska / Grzegorz Maziarczyk (eds.): (Im)perfection Subverted, Reloaded and Networked: Utopian Discourse across Media. 2015.

Vol. 9 Jadwiga Węgrodzka (ed.): Characters in Literary Fictions. 2015.

Vol. 10 Halszka Leleń: H. G. Wells: The Literary Traveller in His Fantastic Short Story Machine. 2016.

Vol. 11 Olena Lytovka: The Uncanny House in Elizabeth Bowen's Fiction. 2016.

www.peterlang.com